GETTING OFF THE TREADMILL

ESCAPING THE RACE TO NOWHERE

Michael J. Lauesen

Russell,
Wishing you many long
beautiful days and good tired nights
Regards,
Mike Lauesen

INDIE BOOKS
INTERNATIONAL

ISBN-10: 1-941870-91-0
ISBN-13: 978-1-941870-91-4
Library of Congress Control Number: 2017937104

Designed by Joni McPherson, mcphersongraphics.com

INDIE BOOKS INTERNATIONAL, LLC
2424 VISTA WAY, SUITE 316
OCEANSIDE, CA 92054
www.indiebooksintl.com

DEDICATION

I dedicate this book to my baseball buddy, my only son, Conor. Your courageous journey through darkness has allowed me to embrace the light of forgiveness, strength, and contribution.

TABLE OF CONTENTS

CHAPTER 1

Trapped on the Treadmill

Have you ever been trapped at an airport because flights were cancelled and you were forced to spend the night? When was the last time you were stuck in your car during rush hour with a heavy rainstorm or snowstorm pounding the roof and windows of your car?

I have lived in Chicago most of my life. Plenty of opportunities for entrapment present themselves every day. It is a busy, vibrant city that counts among its nicknames, according to former mayor Richard J. Daley, "The City That Works." It *is* the city that works, but I believe we work too much.

Growing up in a home where hard work is valued was a blessing. My father, Howard Lauesen, a World War II veteran, worked two full-time jobs for many years to support his growing family. Howard and Blanche (my Mom) raised eight children on a modest income in a three-bedroom ranch home with one bathroom on a busy street. My three older sisters and older brother all worked during high school. I did the same, holding several jobs in high school. Working allowed the Lauesen kids to buy a few necessities like a pair of jeans, dress, or athletic shoes. As an athlete growing up, baseball was and still is my favorite sport. This book, like the rhythm of a well-played baseball game, is nine chapters. A baseball game has nine innings. I hope you enjoy the intricacies of the "game."

Let's start at the beginning and allow me to introduce myself. My name is Michael Lauesen, and I am happily married to my high school sweetheart, Barbara. We have four adult children. I have had several careers in my life. Starting out as a CPA with a large firm, I then became a sales professional and eventually a business founder/owner. Currently, I am a professional speaker and a coach for business owners and Chief Executives in a peer group. As a speaker, I educate, inform, and inspire people on how to find purpose and fulfillment in everyday life. I wrote *Getting off the Treadmill* because I wanted to change people's lives for the better. My main message is, don't live your life in a sleepwalking trance. Instead, be aware of all the joys life has to offer. As a result of these pages, my hope is you'll find more personal insights, more life direction, more happiness, and use the tools included to improve the quality of your life. On a personal note, I am a life-long Chicago Cubs baseball fan, which obviously builds character and patience. My patience was finally rewarded with a World Series Championship in 2016.

As a fifty-nine-year-old white male who grew up in a modest Chicago suburb, I have been healthy and physically fit my entire life. At five-foot-ten-inches, with a medium, muscular build, it takes some effort to maintain this physique. Because I want my wife to continue to think I'm good looking, I keep my gray hair short, as I have lost most of it on the top of my head. My complexion tans easily and seems to complement my blue eyes. I like to smile and laugh, yet can be very intense. Colleagues, friends, and my children have described me as understanding, open to possibilities, and sometimes too sarcastic.

Traveling has been a large part of both my business and personal life. I frequently ride the train when traveling downtown and have always enjoyed, sometimes with silly pleasure, watching folks get on and off the train.

What happens? Inevitably someone gets upset or, as I like to say, gets triggered. On the flip side, I have observed people who are not triggered or upset. They seem to be on autopilot, not observing or noticing the environment or what is going on around them. This is sleepwalking, being zoned out or numb. You may have your own descriptors.

Why is this? Why do commuters sit in the same seats every day? When people walk from the train or walk through an intersection, why are they not paying attention to where they are going? What are they doing? No one seems to *see* what is going on in front, next to, or above him or her.

Have you observed folks walking across a street in your neighborhood with their ear buds in, ignoring the sign that says "Do Not Walk," almost getting hit by a car?

Do they see themselves the way I see them? Do they realize they are often walking through life in a daze, sleepwalking and not paying attention? Do they arrive at their destination without knowing how they got there? Folks seem to be in a race rushing to nowhere.

This reminds me of Harry Chapin, a poet and songwriter who died prematurely. He wrote these lines for his song, *Greyhound:*

> First time I understood
>
> it has got to be the going
>
> not the getting there
>
> that is good.

As Harry so aptly stated, do we enjoy the commute? Do we find energy dashing through the terminal at the airport? How much do we appreciate the opportunity to walk our dogs and bask in the sunlight and fresh air? I have never enjoyed walks as much as recently. My grandson, Luke, was born eleven months ago and I have the opportunity to be with him regularly. I am truly grateful I'm healthy enough to take a walk with Luke. There is nothing else to accomplish but to be present on the walk with my grandson. Do we delight and savor being by ourselves at a park? Can we quiet our minds?

Small children have not learned this numbing, sleepwalking behavior. They live in a "play" state of mind—no clock watching; they don't know or care about time. When you observe small children at play, they are immersed in the activity they are doing. Picture a four-year-old with freckles and red hair, playing with small wooden blocks of various shapes and sizes for endless hours. Imagine two six-year-olds kicking a soccer ball back and forth in a large grassy open field until their parents call for them to come home.

Children notice the smallest things and are often in an *alpha state*.

Alpha state *is a measurement of brain waves. The combination of synchronized electrical activity in the brain is called a brainwave because it is cyclic and wavelike in nature. Brain waves are divided into five different bandwidths. Delta and theta waves occur when we are sleeping or in deep meditation. They are the slowest brain waves. Alpha waves, or the alpha state, are typically created when we daydream or consciously practicing mindfulness or meditation. The alpha state can also be created during aerobic exercise. Beta waves dominate our waking state and are faster brain waves then alpha, theta, or delta. The final brain wave is gamma waves. They're the fastest of brain wave bandwidths. They relate to simultaneous processing of information from different brain areas and are associated with higher states of conscious perception.*

The alpha state is focused, meditative, and includes daydreaming. Children come into the world with a *clean slate* and are not corrupted with prejudice, bias, or judgment. I wonder why we often lose the frequency of the alpha state as we grow up? Is it because we become more socialized? Can we become like small children again? It is possible to do so, and in my opinion is critical to having a significant and fulfilling life.

How often have you seen a mom, dad, or caretaker pushing their baby or toddler in a stroller while talking on a mobile phone? I notice this many times a day in my neighborhood. It is also obvious when traveling. Before cellular devices, it was impossible to talk on a phone and push a stroller at the same time. We took a walk, pushed our baby or toddler, communicated with him or her, and took pleasure in the experience. Nicholas Carr, author of *The Shallows: What the Internet Is Doing to Our Brains*, suggests smartphone use distracts us from paying attention and experiencing reflective moments in daily life. Research shows we use our smartphones up to eighty-five times a day for an average of less than thirty seconds. The total time utilized can be as high as several hours a day.

"Getting off the treadmill" means being mindful and paying attention to what is happening. When you take a walk, actually *take a walk*. When you read a book, *read the book*. When you ride your bike, *ride the bike*. There is no such thing as multitasking.

One of my favorite sayings is "When you do the dishes, do the dishes!" Contemporary Vietnamese monk, Thich Nhat Hanh, a Nobel Peace Prize nominee, says the following: "To my mind, the idea that doing dishes is unpleasant can occur only when you aren't doing them. Once you are standing in front of the sink with your sleeves rolled up and in the warm water, it is really quite pleasant. I enjoy taking my time with each dish, being fully aware of the dish, the water, and each movement of my hands. I know that if I hurry in order to eat dessert sooner, the time of washing dishes will be unpleasant and not worth living. That would be a pity, for each minute, each second of life is a miracle. The dishes themselves and that fact that I am here washing them are miracles!" Thich Nhat Hahn is not on the treadmill of life.

My Mom taught me a wonderful lesson about paying attention and staying off the treadmill of life. She was a voracious reader who always had a novel at her side. It was her time to relax and go to alpha. When I came home from school, Mom always put her book down to visit with me, as she was an active listener. She was focused on me and listened to my stories, joys, and concerns. Whatever I needed to talk about, Mom was always attentive.

As a stay-at-home Mom, she was the backbone of our family. Creative cooking was a skill she mastered because of the necessity of making meals on a meager budget. She was five-foot-six-inches and had a modest weight and frame. Mom had difficulty going up and down the basement stairs to even do laundry with the burden of her bad feet. It was seldom I didn't see her curly brown hair in curlers. The Irish curse of fair skin, easily burned in the sun, was Mom's plight. Because of very poor eyesight, she wore "coke-bottle" eyeglasses. This made her uncomfortable driving a car. Even under these circumstances, Mom had a tremendous wit.

Mom never seemed to be in a hurry. When we visited, she had an amazing ability to make me feel like I was the most important person at that moment. When I left the room, Mom would go back to her book. When Mom died in 1991, our Pastor, Doug, spoke at her committal service at the cemetery. This is what I remember Doug saying: "Blanche traveled through her books. She had bad feet and did not have the financial means to travel. As a result, she never traveled outside the United States." But through novels like *Shogun*, *Noble House*, *Trinity*, *Clan of the Cave Bear*, and *Aztec*, she lived and experienced places she was never able to travel to in person. Through reading, Mom also had a time machine that allowed her to experience much of what life had to offer. She only focused on one thing at a time. She was always present and in the moment. What a true gift she gave to me.

Mom was a mentor to me. Many people have coaches, mentors, and trusted advisors throughout their lives. They are from all phases of our lives. Parents, siblings, teachers, coaches, bosses at work, clergy, and even an encounter with a stranger can have a profound impact. I have had countless mentors in my life. Dad and Mom, my sisters and brothers, my wife Barbara and our children, George Thomas my college baseball coach—all mentored me in countless ways. This list could go on.

Jean Valjean, the protagonist of Victor Hugo's 1862 novel, *Les Miserables,* continues to be an impactful mentor to me. Valjean is an ordinary man attempting to live a normal life after nineteen years in prison for stealing bread to feed his sister's starving children during an economic depression. Jean Valjean's life is drastically altered by the kindness of a priest who forgives him for stealing and more importantly provides him another chance at life. He challenges him to live a life of love, compassion, and faith in God the rest of his living days. What if our life and faith journey displayed more forgiveness, love, and compassion to one another, like Jean Valjean? He was not racing to nowhere. His race was won by the life he led loving others with compassion and grace.

Another preferred quote of mine is, "When the student is ready, the teacher will appear." I was a ready student with countless mentors. I was a grateful mentee. Mentors assist you in getting off the treadmill. Mentors have wisdom and care about you. They are ready to provide advice or just listen. They may approach you positively, with humility, or they may hit you with a two-by-four to get your attention. Both approaches are effective. Timing is the critical component.

Mentors are teachers. One theme of this book is about the lessons we learn in life. I have learned many lessons throughout my life. Stephen Covey's book, *The 7 Habits of Highly Effective People,* has been a bestselling business and self-help book since its release. Covey's book contains much wisdom, many lessons, and healthy habits for everyday life. Habit number two is, "begin with the end in mind." I believe this is the most important habit. Covey asks us to do a revealing exercise: Go to your own funeral. There are four speakers. One is a family member—your spouse, one of your children, a sibling, a cousin. Another is a good friend—someone who has known you for a good length of time. The third speaker is someone from your work or profession. The fourth is from your place of worship or community organization.

What would your family member say? What would he or she talk about? What would your friend say? Would he be reflective about your friendship and how you were there for each other?

My good friend Eugene (Gene) Mahoney's family asked me to speak at his funeral after his untimely death in the summer of 2006. Other than my father's, I had never spoken at a funeral. I talked about Gene's friendship and how much I learned every time I spoke or was with Gene. His brilliant and thought-provoking mind was a defining characteristic. He was my personal and business attorney and I feel his influence even today. He was an amazing friend and mentor in my life.

What would the person from your church say? Were you committed to your church? Did you live a faithful life? Since my kids were toddlers, I have had a devoted relationship to my church. The last several years, I have been in a significant leadership role. I would hope someone from the church would talk about my faith, how it blossomed and grew over time, and the impact the church was for my family and me.

What would you want each speaker to say?

This is a profound and powerful exercise. I encourage you to think hard about it. If you died today, who would the four speakers be? We will discuss this more in the next chapter.

This book entails many themes. I will share some of the countless things I've learned along the way, including how we can find meaning and uncover our purpose in life, understand the mystery of faith, the divine, and how they are interwoven regularly. You will develop your own tool kit to assist you in navigating life and to find more fulfillment, joy, and purpose in the mundane and the spiritual. I will offer practical suggestions based on values of humility, gratitude, paying attention, and daily reflection. I will share specific personal life experiences and experiences of many other people. Some folks are famous; most are ordinary like me.

In the end, this book should be read as if you are attending a baseball game. Just as there is no time limit in baseball, there is no time limit to finish the book. There is also no time limit incorporating the lessons and tools in this book.

Hopefully these lessons, stories, tools, and exercises will make you think, laugh, and even cry. Maybe they will empower you to change your life. Likely, my life journey has been similar to yours. There have been wonderful moments, sad moments, and times of exploring the nature of who we are and why we are here.

My goal for this book is to provide you a foundation or buttress to further your footing for a meaningful and fulfilling life allowing you a restful sleep each and every day.

We can actually live the life we want. When you are ready to get off the treadmill, a teacher will appear. You will become a student, always learning. I hope you will be my student throughout the remainder of this book. Every person we come in contact with influences us in some way. It is our choice.

It is never too late to get off the treadmill and the race to nowhere so you can realize an intentional, fulfilling, and purposeful life. Are you ready to get off the treadmill?

CHAPTER 2

Uncovering Your Life *Purpose*

What is your life purpose and why is it so important? The dictionary definition of "purpose" is:

1. The reason for which something is done, made, used, etc.

2. An intended or desired result; end; aim; goal.

3. To have a purpose.

I like definition number one: The reason for which something is done, made, used. This is a simple explanation, yet determining your life purpose is challenging and is fluid over our life. How do you determine or uncover your life's purpose? Why do you get up in the morning? If most people took the time to think deeply about this question, it is possible they would discover their life's purpose.

The answer might be found in your career, home life, spirituality, relationships, and/or family life. No matter where you focus, your life purpose includes every aspect of your life. It is the foundation for everyday living. A profound question to ask is: why am I here on this earth?

This chapter will provide examples of how you can determine your own purpose in life. Once we know our purpose, we can begin to lead an intentional and fulfilling life.

It isn't easy. What is holding you back? Are you on the treadmill, sleepwalking through life? Have you started a race without a finish line? Are you too busy? I appreciate the term *being busy*. Being busy often denotes we have accomplished much in a day, week, or even a month. Productivity may be the opposite of busy. Author and professor Brené Brown suggests, in a series of lectures, that we equate being busy with being productive. Often it is a badge of honor to work long hours trying to further our careers. There are countless stories of people who are exhausted at the end of each day only to repeat the whole process every day without any self-reflection or purpose. Are they racing to nowhere?

Bill Murray's character (Phil Connors) in the movie *Groundhog Day* is *racing to nowhere*. Phil is not a likable person. He is self-centered and focused only on what he feels is important for his career. As the movie unfolds, Phil wakes up and realizes, incredulously, it's the *same* day as it was yesterday. This continues day after day after day. Phil attempts crazy things to end the repeating Groundhog Day. He stays up late and tries not to fall asleep. He eventually falls asleep, wakes up and, sadly, (tragic comedy) it is the same day again. Smashing the alarm clock to bits and pieces one evening, Phil believes without the alarm clock working, he will break this crazy, unexplainable cycle. Unfortunately, this strategy fails and he wakes up to the perfectly ringing clock the next morning.

He soon understands, after many days of frustration, Phil Connors has no future. He does not know his *purpose*. Nothing changes. Phil can predict what will happen specifically each day because he has lived each day many times over and over. These daily memories are embedded in his being. He has the same encounters with the same people, at the exact time every day. One of them is a child in a tree. The child falls from the tree, and Phil catches him and prevents him from falling to the ground. He encounters a sickly homeless man, but does not help him and the man dies. The next day he sees him again, even though he died the previous day. The homeless man actually dies every night in spite of Phil's efforts. Each day, Phil is doomed to repeat Groundhog Day until he gets it right. Are we repeating our own Groundhog Day?

Rita, played by Andie MacDowell, is the main female role in the movie. Phil attempts various methods to be intimate with Rita. In one scene, he discovers all her passions and interests and painstakingly educates himself about each and every one of these. This technique, as well as others, reveals Phil is a fraud and not a sincere person. He is devastated. Groundhog Day will return again tomorrow. After several weeks, he gradually realizes life is not about operating in a self-serving world, using manipulation to achieve what we want or going through the motions of life without being genuinely present. Phil is on the treadmill and the race to nowhere. Numb, with no idea what to do next, Phil is a lost soul.

Eventually, Phil's epiphany comes. Phil becomes a kind, caring, and wonderful human being. He chooses to live each, moment to its fullest and be immensely present each day. Phil embraces each day, and soon his *groundhog days* are over.

Phil uncovers his new life purpose: to be present, focused, and to pay attention to every detail a day has to offer. Kindness and making a difference in the world is important. Each time I watch *Groundhog Day*, I am reminded to be present and to live each day to its fullest.

To further understand life's purpose, consider the following visual and writing experience as a vehicle to uncover your mission or purpose in life. Imagine you are attending a close friend's funeral. As the funeral progresses, you are shocked to realize it is your funeral! In chapter one, we introduced the four speakers at your funeral.

TOOL BOX

YOUR OWN FUNERAL

1. Decide the four people who will speak at your funeral (Family member, close friend, colleague from your career, a member of your place of worship or civic organization).

    a. Family Member:

    _____

    b. Close Friend:

    _____

    c. Career Colleague:

    _____

    d. Worship Place/Civic Organization:

    _____

2. Write what each person will say about you.

    a. Family Member:

    _____

    _____

    _____

    _____

    _____

_____

_____

b. Close Friend:

_____

_____

_____

_____

_____

_____

c. Career Colleague:

_____

_____

_____

_____

_____

_____

d. Worship Place/Civic Organization:

_____

_____

_____

_____

_____

_____

_____

3. Below is a vertical line and two horizontal lines. To the left of the vertical line, put the year you were born.

4. Now I want you to think about the year you will die. Is it twenty, thirty, or perhaps forty years or more from today? Envision a ripe old age of ninety, 100, or beyond. To the right of the second horizontal line, write the year you think you will die.

_____ | _____

5. In the space below titled "Life So Far," list your most satisfying accomplishments and experiences, both personally and professionally. Itemize your biggest disappointments. Take your time; there are no correct answers.

Life So Far _____

_____

_____

_____

_____

_____

6. In the space below titled "The Time that Remains," begin to write what you hope to have experienced and/or accomplished. A few examples might be: births of grandchildren, getting married or remarried, vacations you will take, relocating to a new home and or city, becoming an entrepreneur, or retiring with a specific age in mind. Make note of why this is important to you. It is critical to write your thoughts on the above, as this enables you to uncover your purpose for the remaining time we have here on earth.

The Time that Remains_____

_____

_____

_____

_____

_____

Additionally, there is a very important question to reflect on as you try to determine your purpose. How do you spend your free time? There seems to be judgment in our culture around taking naps or having an unstructured day where we plan on doing nothing. As I mentioned earlier, working long hours can be a badge of honor for some individuals.

What we actually do with our free time can tell a significant amount about us as individuals. Do you have free time? What do you do with your free time? Do you and can you relax? Reading a good novel, watching a movie or TV show, enjoying time with your family and close friends are possibilities. Is working at a soup kitchen or volunteering at your church something you might do? How about meditating, praying, or physically working out?

Here's another tool: Take a few minutes to reflect on how you spend the time you aren't working and sleeping. These exercises will help to determine your life purpose.

TOOL BOX

WHAT I DO IN MY FREE TIME

_____

_____

_____

_____

_____

_____

_____

_____

_____

This is not as easy as it sounds. Living and leading a fulfilling and enjoyable life with a definable purpose is obtainable. Knowing your purpose or mission enters you in a race in which you control the outcome and the finish line.

Another route to identify your life's purpose is asking yourself a question: What is the *Why* in my life? What do I believe in? The Simon Sinek TED talk, "How Great Leaders Inspire Action," explains the Why. I encourage you to watch it at www.ted.com/talks/simon_sinek_ how_great_leaders_inspire_action. This eighteen-minute video may change your life. I challenge you to watch it once a month for three months. You will discover more significance with each viewing.

The Why is our passion and what we truly believe in. It is our purpose and mission. Your mission or purpose can start with articulating and writing what you care about. Write all the things in life you care about. Think of the things you are passionate about. A theme will reveal itself through your note-taking. This theme becomes your purpose. It gets you up in the morning; it's your beacon of light and grounds you daily.

WHAT I CARE ABOUT

Through adversity and challenging times, you may question your life purpose. When this happens, returning to your life purpose will center you and bring you back to why you are here. I get up each morning with two fundamental purposes: the first, giving back all the love I have received; the other, making a positive difference in every person I meet. Today, these are my core purposes. Over time, my purpose has evolved. I am privileged and fortunate to have an altruistic purpose. Human beings' purpose throughout the world evolve and may even be "ordinary." It might be providing for their family, finding work, or just surviving another day. One's purpose could be graduating from various levels of school. The journey and the effort are critical. Creating daily reminders of your purpose is extremely helpful. When I remember to focus on my core purpose by praying, practicing gratefulness, reading meditations, or quiet yoga time, it centers me. These practices of mindful attention allow me to do the very best I can in making a positive and significant difference in every life I encounter. When you think of core purpose, imagine how purpose can be revealed to each of us.

This revealing of purpose is highlighted in the book *Good to Great,* by Jim Collins. He references a longitudinal study of trauma, significant adversity, and tragedy in individual lives. Three outcomes arise.

One outcome is the individual never recovers fully from the adversity that could result from the death of a parent, child, health issues, divorce, losing your job...the list goes on. When a life is impacted so significantly we are changed forever; our life trajectory is dangerously altered.

The second outcome is more favorable. A person goes through the grief of the tragedy, then gets back to her life without a significant change. We see this often. A loved one dies or divorces and life goes on, or cancer is discovered and successfully treated. Unlike outcome one, even though it is difficult, a person recovers and gets back to normal everyday life. This may take weeks, months, or even years.

The third outcome from significant challenges and trauma is not only an eventual recovery but also an opportunity for growth: working through trauma can in fact be full of life-changing possibilities. Our destiny is actually changed moving forward. Our mission or purpose in life can be revealed as a result of the misfortune. There are many examples of this outcome. Let us take a look at a few internationally infamous *real-life* stories:

- The Taliban shot **Malala Yousafzai**, an adolescent Pakistani student, in the face after she spoke out for education rights for girls. After recovering, she spoke to the U.N. Youth Assembly on her 16th birthday in July, 2013. Through this adversity, she is now committed to fighting for educational equity for Muslim girls and women. She has created a foundation to support education for Muslim women. I would suggest this is Malala's life purpose. Malala was able to transform her own life and the lives of many other Muslim girls and women.

- **Christopher Reeve**, who played Superman in the 1978 big-screen adaptation, was paralyzed after being thrown from his horse. Before his death in 2004, Mr. Reeve started a foundation for assisting people with spinal cord injuries. One of the missions of the foundation is currently funding a program in developing a revolutionary electrical stimulation device, allowing individuals the ability to walk who were told they would never walk again. From the seeds of this terrible accident, Christopher Reeve found purpose in finding a cure for spinal cord injuries.

- **Candy Lightner** took on a public fight against drunken driving. Lightner founded MADD (Mothers Against Drunk Driving) in 1980 after a repeat drunk-driving offender killed her daughter, Cari. The mission and purpose of MADD is to stop drunk driving, support the victims of this violent crime, and prevent underage drinking. Waking up each morning, Candy believes she can eliminate drunk driving and thousands of senseless deaths.

- Most recently, the story of **Pete Frates** inspired me. Suffering from the progressive plight of ALS (sometimes called "Lou Gehrig's Disease"), Pete Frates was instrumental in starting the Ice

Bucket Challenge, a fundraising and awareness campaign for ALS. The challenge entails pouring a large bucket of freezing ice water over your head, which runs down and covers your entire body. The day he was diagnosed, Pete told his family that he envisioned billionaire Bill Gates, founder of Microsoft, doing the ice bucket challenge. Sometime later, Pete's dream was actualized. Bill Gates did partake in the ice bucket challenge. Pete's mom, Nancy Frates, has a TED talk that is inspirational, emotional and motivational: www.ted.com/talks/nancy_frates_why_my_family_started_the_als_ice_bucket_challenge_the_rest_is_history. Pete and Nancy found purpose through this horrendous terminal disease.

- Another example is **Nelson Mandela**. Mr. Mandela was sentenced to life in prison for committing sabotage against South Africa's apartheid government. He had an awakening and a defining moment when he decided to be part of the solution to end racism and blatant discrimination. He helped end apartheid and became a recognized world leader for peace, justice and human rights.

- **Dan Baker's** book, *What Happy People Know*, tells a poignant and compelling story about a founder and CEO of an engineering firm. He lost his whole company during the 9/11 attacks on the World Trade Center in New York City. One year prior, he had lost his wife to breast cancer. His daughter coerced him to visit Canyon Ranch, a health and wellness spa in Tucson, Arizona, in an attempt to help him recover from his deep sadness and depression. During a meeting with the therapist at Canyon Ranch, he shared his son had also died in the collapsed tower. His son worked with him at the firm.

Understandably, he was drinking heavily and was severely depressed. Although it did not happen overnight, he eventually started a foundation to support families devastated by the 9/11 tragedies. He successfully turned toward doing something significant and inspiring. He found new purpose in his life through several devastating tragedies.

- An additional calamitous story is from bestselling author **Rabbi Harold Kushner**, who wrote *When Bad Things Happen to Good People* as a catharsis for himself. His son was diagnosed with a premature aging disease at three years of age. The doctors told Rabbi Kushner his son would not live beyond his early teenage years. He did not anticipate his book would become an international bestseller. How we react and cope with "bad things" is critical. In discovering bad things happen to good and bad people, Rabbi Kushner suggests the power of prayer in our community, family, and friends as one way of dealing with tragedy. He has written several books and continues to inspire and console thousands of people.

Next, I want to delve into a more personal story of trauma and transformation. My wife Barbara and I have friends who have lost children because of accidents or disease. Burying one of your children must be one of the saddest things in life. The intimate devastation eludes most words or descriptions. I am not sure if a person can ever fully recover from the loss of a child. As our friend, Sue Walsh, a mother who survived this very tragedy, stated, *"none of this is ever planned, and you never fully recover."*

Sue and Brian Walsh are friends Barbara and I have known since high school. We live in the same neighborhood in a suburb of Chicago. We raised our children through the same primary and high schools. Brian and Sue have three children. Bradley, their oldest, was two years older than our son, Conor. Conor was a friend of Brad, played with Brad, and looked up to him when they were in primary school. I remember fondly the numerous requests from Brad and Conor to blast the song "Walk of Life" by Dire Straits. Conor and Brad jumped and flipped countless times over and around the brown sectional in the basement of our home as the music blared. To this day, the joy of this song immediately inspires many memories.

Brian is a grandpa, father, master carpenter, plumber, cabinetmaker, and someone who can build a house from the foundation up with his own hands. From a large Irish Catholic family of eleven, Brian is the second-oldest. He is an artist who works with wood, marble, Corian, and other building substrates. On his six-foot, solidly built frame, Brian has a welcoming smile, an engaging sense of humor, a sensitive and emotional face, kind blue eyes, and strength beyond his strong physical presence. Brian is most comfortable building and creating sacred spaces in his frequently worn denim overalls.

Sue is a mom, grandmother, nurse practitioner, D.N.P. (doctor of nursing practice), and the quintessential caretaker. Sue is five-foot-six with a slight build, a fair complexion, and short blond hair. Her eyes portray emotion beyond their blue hue. A welcoming and compassionate spirit for all people, Sue defines kindness. Sue never planned on the profound impact of the book *The Purpose-driven Life: What on Earth Am I Here For?* by Rick Warren, which she finished reading in early 2003. After Sue completed the book, she pondered becoming a medical missionary one day.

Little did Sue and Brian know that the book would have such significance so soon. In the early morning hours on May 18, 2003, Bradley, their son, died in a late-night motorcycle accident at twenty-one years of age. Hearing the tragic news first thing in the morning, we hurried to their home. It was the saddest day Barbara and I ever experienced. What do you say? What can you say? We hugged them and told them we loved them and we were so very sorry for this terrible accident. Families and friends came to their home for many days. At the time, Brad's sister Maggie was nineteen and his brother Kyle was seventeen. The endless grieving began as the tragedy was so unsettling and could not be articulated.

For months, Sue and Brian courageously consoled their large extended family of many siblings and over thirty nephews and nieces, along with many of Brad's friends. Sue had been suffering from sleepless nights and was likely experiencing post-traumatic stress disorder. She repeatedly told Brian losing Brad was the worst possible thing that could have happened in life. However, after months of profound sadness, Brian firmly and gently placed Sue's face in both his finely leathered, calloused hands and said, "No Susie, losing you would be the worst thing to happen." Brian was the rock she needed; she for him as well. He is the foundation of her strength and resiliency. When Brad died, Brian lost not just a son, but also a friend, a fellow tradesman, and a future business partner.

As we talked recently, Sue said she deeply regrets returning to work as a nurse several weeks after Brad's death. She had little time to mourn Brad's death because she was taking care of everyone else. Over the next few months, Sue gift-wrapped over 100 copies of *The Purpose-driven Life*. She wanted all Brad's friends and others to find meaning in the terrible tragedy. Her faith reminded her heaven was a real place. She finished the last thank-you notes for Brad's wake and funeral in December, seven months after Brad's death. Days later, an auto hit Sue as she walked across the street; she was leaving work at the hospital, trying to live the routines of her daily life. The impact of the car fractured her right leg and knee, injured her left hip and left shoulder, and sprained both wrists. For three months, she could not place any weight on her leg and was not able to drive for six months. As Sue reflected, she described this sedentary time as a God moment. "Be still and know that I am God!" This kind of divine presence will be explored more closely throughout the book.

With the loss of Brad, Sue and Brian were unsteady and reeling. As Sue convalesced, she understood being bedridden and still were gifts allowing her to pray, sit with the pain, and heal both body and soul. Sue eventually discovered even though her life was tragically changed forever, there was still joy to be found, every day and everywhere.

Brian and Sue have a profoundly rich life. Sue finished her Doctor of Nursing Practice (D.N.P.) several years after Brad's passing, and Brian continues to be a master carpenter. Their children are happy and settled. Their son Kyle was married last summer in their back yard. What a joyous celebration and blessing. What a privilege to be part of the ceremony. It was especially meaningful as we remembered Brad's post-funeral gathering in the same back yard. Tragic, incredible!

Out of this tragedy, Brian and Sue created a nonprofit organization, Little by Little in 2007 (. www.littlebylittle. org). The mission of Little by Little is "Faithfully partnering with those in need of improved health and well-being." Sue and Brian travel several times a year to Haiti, providing much-needed medical care in a very low-resourced village near Port-Au-Prince. Teaching at the University of Illinois College of Nursing triggered Sue's initial purpose for trips to Haiti—providing service learning for nurse practitioners.

In January 2010, Brian and Sue were in Haiti with a team of twenty-three volunteers when a devastating earthquake hit the island. Their medical team unexpectedly became first-responders, caring for thousands of critically injured and dying people of all ages over the course of four days. Not surprisingly, Sue and Brian seemed to have more emotional capacity for such tragedy than others on their team. A few years prior, they had experienced the death of Brad, the worst parental fear imaginable. They survived both the earthquake in Haiti and their previously broken hearts. Their marriage, family, friendships, and purpose for life only grew stronger. After the catastrophic earthquake, Sue wrote a book about the experience: *Walking in Broken Shoes*.

Sue believes purpose is critically important in life. Brad's death was a tragedy and knocked her out of balance and into deep suffering. Her Christian belief in heaven was aroused. Was Brad's death for naught? Convalescing for six months from her accident, her core beliefs reemerged and brought her life gradually back in balance. Sue continues to share her story in numerous ways through her career, foundation, speaking engagements, and her book.

~

I know these examples are extreme. They demonstrate that life is fragile, difficult, and filled with tragedies. Tragedies lead us to a choice. Brian and Sue Walsh chose to share their story of tragedy and belief in life after death. Through terrible adversities and challenges, each person discussed found a new purpose and mission. I do not share these stories to suggest we all need a life tragedy or significant life challenge to reveal our purpose moving forward. However, we *should* spend time with ourselves and think about our greater purpose in life.

All of us have various purposes which evolve over our lifetimes. My main purpose after Barbara and I were married was raising a family. We wanted to provide all the opportunities necessary for our children to be well educated, healthy, and successful adults in the game of life.

Mahatma Gandhi said, "If we could change ourselves, the tendencies in the world would also change. As a man changes his own nature, so does the attitude of the world change towards him. We need not wait to see what others do." Another way of saying this is, "Be the change you wish to see in the world."

Uncovering your life's purpose can be a lifelong process. Now that you have started to explore your life purpose, are you ready to continue the journey with me?

CHAPTER THREE

Pay Attention

Now it is time to get off the treadmill and create a tool kit for your life.

My father, a strong, proud, and sensitive man was a lather, which is similar to a carpenter. Dad went to work each morning with his tool kit. When he arrived at the job site, he removed the tool belt from the trunk of the car and diligently examined the tools. Dad then placed the belt low around his waist. Some of his tools included a blueprint, level, hammer, magnifying glass, and retractable tape measure. Dad's ability to read a blueprint, however, was his most important tool. It was obvious to me how critical these tools were to him. He cared and valued them. This was his life's profession.

I fondly and clearly remember, when I worked with Dad one summer, the pride he demonstrated in the artistry of lathing. His tools were paramount in successfully completing the job. Without them, my father would not have been the man I grew to love and respect. We cannot live our lives without our own tool kit to navigate life's joys, challenges, and sorrows. Similar to how my father needed tools to do his job, we each need tools in our own daily lives to escape the race to nowhere.

The next five chapters encompass developing these five tools for our own life journey. These tools, though often analogous to chosen objects are: *Pay Attention (blueprint), Utilize Goals (level), Start Simply (hammer), Reflect Daily (magnifying glass or microscope),* and *Forgive (retractable tape measure).*

The first tool required in our kit for life is *Pay Attention.* Let's start at the very beginning. I met Dr. Doug Runnells during high school at my wife Barbara's church. Doug was an English professor at the University of Michigan before he attended divinity school and became a pastor. Doug is brilliant, with a capacious mind. He served ten years at Barbara's family's church and more than ten years at our church, the Glenview Community church. In 1980, he married us. As you can undoubtedly surmise, Doug has played a significant role in our life. Over the years, our entire family has had many in-depth conversations regarding his articulate, challenging, inspirational, and thought-provoking sermons.

As we learned from one of Doug's sermons, his first law of spirituality is paying attention.

The dictionary defines attention as:

1. A concentration of the mind on a single object or thought, especially one preferentially

selected from a complex, with a view to limiting or clarifying receptivity by narrowing the range of stimuli.

2. A capacity to maintain selective or sustained concentration.

Focusing on sustained concentration serves us well. Doug's nonnegotiable first law of spirituality is the need to focus and have sustained concentration. There are infinite ways to describe paying attention, such as becoming completely focused or being "in the zone."

That being said, it is one of the most difficult things to incorporate in your everyday life. Why? Because we live in a world of divided attention. We multitask and infrequently focus on one thing at a time. Paying attention requires significant effort. The contemporary digital world we live in inundates us with thousands of messages a day, including text messages, e-mails, news flashes on Twitter, Facebook, and e-mail alerts. The daily advertising we see in the digital world, print world, and the media world is 24/7. It is extremely difficult in today's society to *Pay Attention* and stay focused in the moment: distraction is ubiquitous. Being present in the moment is to be in the zone.

Have you ever met someone with a peaceful presence who actively listens as if you were the most important person in the world? I have met very few people like this in my life. Their feeling of calmness and tranquility inspire me. There is a spiritual quality about them.

They know how to pay attention and be "in the moment" much of their day.

Many people have written about meditation and paying attention over the years. Eckhart Tolle wrote a book, *The Power of Now,* which is a wonderful read. One of my favorite suggestions from this book takes place while meditating or praying; It is easy to forget the mind remains highly active even within a quiet and meditative state. We think of many thoughts not relevant to our meditation. Tolle suggests seeing or feeling these thoughts as if they are clouds passing through our mind. Release the thoughts without judgment. Then return to paying attention and your meditative state.

Eckhart Tolle discusses a collective consciousness throughout the world. What kind of world would we live in if everyone was peaceful, calm, and authentically present in each and every moment? Perhaps, some kind of peace throughout the world may indeed be possible.

Because of this, getting off the treadmill fundamentally first occurs through the act of paying attention. It is achieved by meditating, praying, and opening up to the possibilities of slowing down your mind.

A business group I participated in eighteen years ago invited Steven Snyder, author of *Focused Passion,* to speak at one of our monthly meetings. His workshop, which continues today, is about going to your peaceful, quiet place, or alpha state. Through Snyder's workshop and personal practice, I learned to quiet my mind and go to my own peaceful, quiet place. Steven explained the unconscious mind does not know the difference between the real world and the imaginary world. Your peaceful, quiet place, or alpha state, can be real or imaginary. It can be a combination of real and pretend. It may be a beautiful vacation place you visited where you add your own imaginative items.

Through Steven's profound articulations, I was enlightened and permanently impacted. Steven suggests mindfully going to your peaceful, quiet place throughout your day. Any length of time is appropriate: twenty seconds or twenty minutes. Release stress as you quietly breathe, feel, see and listen experiencing your own peaceful, quiet place in your mind—your unconscious mind. This is a form of prayer and meditation. It allows us to be focused and concentrate on something that isn't in our physical, visual, and auditory surroundings.

As Steven further explained, everyone learns in different ways. Some of us are more visual, others auditory, and some are kinesthetic learners. There are a small percentage of people who learn all three ways, but most of us learn using two techniques or styles.

Although much research has been done on types and styles of learning, I will provide a brief recap.

- **Visual learning** necessitates seeing. You use your sight in learning, and this includes more than just viewing pictures and your surroundings. Visual learners utilize charts, graphs, diagrams, and videos. Most waking hours, we see a multitude of videos. YouTube is one of the highest rated websites. When was the last time you watched a video on your smartphone, tablet, or computer? Often, visual learners take and use notes.

- **Kinesthetic learning** requires doing. It can involve physical activity. We use words like "connected" and "feel." It is hands-on learning. Consider how young children navigate iPads and other handheld tablets or smartphones. Fly-fishing depends on kinesthetic learning; you have to perform the activity to acquire the skill.

- **Auditory learning** involves excellent listening. Listening to a book on tape is an example of auditory learning. Listening to a lecture is also auditory learning. Have you ever met a person who listens extremely well? If they are a high auditory learner, they remember a significant portion of what they hear.

After I heard Steven Snyder speak for the first time, I shared this practice with my family. Saying good night to my six-year-old daughter, Taylor, I explained the unconscious mind and alpha.

Taylor and I went to our own peaceful, quiet places for several nights before bedtime. I imagined a peaceful, quiet place where we had vacationed in Kaanapali beach, in Maui, Hawaii. It was a gorgeous day as I sat on the ninth-floor balcony in the condo we'd rented. My thoughts led me to seeing and hearing the sounds of a peregrine falcon flying overhead. Hearing the rain fall in the rainforest on another side of the mountain, seeing as well as feeling the heat of the sun and the balmy breeze on my skin, I was calm and tranquil. It was beautiful, serene, and peaceful. I did not ask Taylor to share the place she visited during the evenings we went to our peaceful, quiet place.

Several days later, we visited our peaceful, quiet place together. We simultaneously opened our eyes and Taylor's piercing blue eyes looked up at me with tears rolling down her cheeks. I asked her what was wrong? She told me she couldn't see anything. "It was dark," she shouted out. "I couldn't find my peaceful, quiet place!"

Taylor was stressed: she could not visualize a place. Although I did not plan on this response, I was prepared from Steven's workshop. Empathizing with Taylor, I suggested everyone hears, feels, and visualizes our own peaceful, quiet place in unique and wonderful ways. Some of us see our place clearly or hear the ocean or the wind or the birds. Others sense it, feeling grounded and connected to their place as kinesthetic learners do. I reassured Taylor there is no correct method to go to your peaceful, quiet place or pay attention. Darkness was as peaceful as it gets.

~

A question to ponder: is focused concentration or paying attention learned or innate? Are we born with the gift or is it learned? We can be trained and conditioned to better focus and pay attention. The potential is there to be taught *not* to pay attention. It is possible for us to attain the skill and gift whether it is inherited or not. Could it be the joy, trauma, pain, and obstacles in life are a true blessing for us to learn and grow from and *Pay Attention*? Clearly life's experiences demonstrate the significance of paying attention. If we make the choice to pay attention and continue to learn and grow, we become better human beings in the process.

As mentioned earlier, my Mom had a gift of paying attention. I don't know whether Mom learned this or was born this way; it did not matter. Mom knew how to visit and *Pay Attention*. She had a distinct, witty, dry sense of humor. Faithfully, Mom had a book in front of her, an Old Milwaukee beer in one hand, and a cigarette between the fingers of her other hand. Coming home from college, sharing the many things I had learned, she set her book aside and listened attentively. Visiting one day, as I rambled on about something, Mom never interrupted, actively listened, focused, and paid attention only to me. When I completed my monologue, she responded with wit and wisdom. Mom listened without judgment. She gave me a gift resonating even today. I follow my instincts, *Pay Attention*, and keep a sense of humor.

~

Psychologist Mihaly Csikszentmihalyi's famous investigations of "optimal experience" have revealed what makes an experience genuinely satisfying is a state of consciousness called "flow." He discusses his research and "flow" in his book, *Flow: The Psychology of Optimal Experience* and a TED talk. He conducted over eight thousand interviews with surgeons, Dominican monks, Himalayan climbers, Navajo shapers, and various athletes. Regardless of culture, where they grew up, education level, and other markers, Csikszentmihalyi outlines seven conditions that are present when a person is in flow.

The seven conditions are:

1. Completely involved in what we are doing—focused, concentrated.

2. A sense of ecstasy and/or being outside of everyday reality.

3. Great in your clarity—knowing what needs to be done, and how well we are doing.

4. Knowing that the activity is doable—that our skills are adequate to the task.

5. A sense of serenity—no worries about oneself, and a feeling of growing beyond the boundaries of the ego.

6. Timelessness—fairly focused on the present,

time seems to pass by in minutes.

7. Intrinsic motivation—whatever produces "flow" becomes its own reward.

Here is an example where "flow" enters the workforce. Masaru Ibuka started Sony Corporation without a product and only an idea. His purpose in starting Sony was "To establish a workplace where engineers can feel the joy of technological innovation, be aware of their mission to society, and to work to their hearts' content." What a breathtaking vision and purpose to start a company! How fortunate to experience "flow" every day at work.

Visualize a Y- and X-axis graph. The Y-axis is labelled "Challenge," and the X-axis is labeled, "Skills." According to Csikszentmihalyi, with higher challenge and higher skill, we can achieve "flow" more easily. If your duties in your career, performing in an athletic event, strenuous exercise, enjoyable yet intense reading, etc. are challenging and require skill, reaching the "flow" state is within your grasp. Playing a demanding card game like bridge may bring you into a "flow" state. Hitting a baseball and running with the ball in football were "flow" states in high school and college for me. Today, taking a long, strenuous, hilly bike ride on rolling country roads brings me to "flow." Reading an interesting historical novel brings me to a "flow" state. Each time I return to the book, picking up where I left off, the "flow" state returns. Writing this book has routinely brought me to a "flow" state.

What brings you to your "flow" and/or alpha state?

There are countless methods and means to achieving a peaceful, present, and concentrated state. For many religions, it is prayer, and for some meditation. It may be going to your alpha or "flow" state. How do we become better? We can practice. It takes perfect practice, not just practice. Perfect practice comes from excellent coaching. I like to use golf as an example of perfect practice. Let's assume I have a flawed swing. If I continue to practice with a flawed swing, the result is not continuous improvement, but the continued frustration of not playing better golf. We need qualified coaching to be taught. If we are not coached or taught legitimate ways to golf, we will never improve our score. As with golf, it is essential to receive proper coaching to meditate and *Pay Attention*.

TOOL BOX

PAYING ATTENTION AND THE ALPHA STATE

Follow each step, in order. You are now starting a coaching lesson.

1. Write all the ways you currently *Pay Attention* during your waking hours.

_____

_____

_____

_____

_____

_____

2. Write the activities that allow you to experience alpha or "flow."

_____

_____

_____

_____

_____

_____

_____

3. Take a deep breath. Imagine your peaceful, quiet place. (When you first imagine your peaceful, quiet place, it is the first place that comes to your mind. Trust your first thought or your intuition.) Describe and write the place. Create written details around your peaceful, quiet place.

_____

_____

_____

_____

_____

_____

4. Practice daily, paying attention during your waking hours, and go to your peaceful, quiet place (alpha state) six to twelve times a day. Twenty seconds is all you need.

5. Create daily reminders for yourself to remember to go to alpha. This could be when you drink water; transitioning from standing and/or sitting to walking; when you enter your car, or the train on your commute. Before you eat or go to bed is also a good reminder to go to alpha.

As mentioned, my peaceful, quiet place is in Maui, and it is raining on one side and the sun is out on another. A peregrine falcon is my favorite bird, and I wanted a peregrine to be in my peaceful, quiet place. Where is your peaceful, quiet place? Is it real or imaginary? Do you feel it, see it and hear the sounds in your peaceful, quiet place? How can we learn to love our quiet place? This peaceful place allows us to be more present and *Pay Attention*, which is our first tool. We no longer race to nowhere when we value and utilize our first tool. Can you begin to pay attention daily? Will you go to your peaceful, quiet place throughout the day? Please continue on with me as the next tool we add to our tool kit is utilizing goals.

CHAPTER FOUR

Utilize Goals

The second tool in our tool kit is *Utilizing Goals*. Although my Dad needed all his tools to complete the job, the most critical one was his ability to read a blueprint. Without the skill of reading it, Dad could not have laid out the job and visualized what needed to be done. The blueprint was necessary for the successful use of his other tools. As a conscientious and productive lather, this was my Dad's foundation.

With Pay Attention as our foundation, we can move on to our next tool, Utilizing Goals. Dad used a level every day. A level is a tool to construct walls and corners proportionally. It creates symmetry and balance. A level floor, then walls, ceiling, and roof are now in equilibrium. Goals accomplish the same, by creating specific, balanced steps in proportion to reach the roof, or end goal. Goals keep us balanced like a level and on the correct track to realize our aspirations in life and get off the treadmill.

To get off the treadmill, we need to *Utilize Goals*.

The dictionary definition of a goal is:

1. The result or achievement toward which effort is directed

2. An aim; an end

Let us focus on definition number one, the result or achievement toward which effort is directed.

Bob Richards, former Olympic gold medalist, spoke about goals at a motivational symposium in 1980, during my college years. At this life-changing event, goal-setting and utilizing goals became a priority for me. Richards won the Olympic pole vault gold medal in 1952 and 1956. To this day, I smile reflecting on his commercials for Wheaties. He would do handstand push-ups while stating, "Wheaties is the breakfast of champions." As the first athlete on the cover of the Wheaties cereal box, he was the General Mills spokesperson for all their cereals from 1956 till 1970. Bob Richards is a motivational speaker, an ordained minister, and currently lives in Waco, Texas, on a ranch with his wife of fifty-four years.

As is often with life-altering events, it was pure serendipity that my wife Barbara and I attended Bob Richards' motivational talk. We eagerly accepted a last-minute invite from Barbara's sister. Bruce (now Caitlyn) Jenner had won the 1976 modern decathlon and was also scheduled to speak. As an athlete at the University of Minnesota, I was excited to hear Bruce Jenner, the "greatest athlete," as the decathlon world champion was commonly referred to. I knew about

Bob Richards because of Wheaties cereal.

Bruce Jenner spoke first. He discussed his decathlon gold medal and the years of training required to win the gold medal. I don't remember much of his talk, although I am sure it had many memorable moments.

Then Bob Richards took the podium and immediately captivated the audience. His jet-black hair complemented his chiseled face and bright eyes. With clearly defined muscles and a barrel chest from years of pole-vaulting, he reminded me what an Olympic athlete looked like. Mr. Richards has probably given hundreds if not thousands of inspirational and motivational speeches throughout his career. I never anticipated the life-changing speech he gave that day. The over-capacity crowd was in for a life-transforming speech. Although this day is embedded in my heart and mind, I have no way of knowing the impact his speech had on other attendees.

Some forty years later, I remember the four guideposts for motivation that defined his speech. I have passionately discussed these topics for many years with family, friends, my own children, and kids I have coached.

Here are the guideposts:

1. Set goals and write them down.

2. Be willing to pay the price for those goals.

3. Believe you deserve great things to happen to you.

4. Allow the possibility you may not achieve your goals.

Mr. Richards used many sports metaphors throughout his talk. He discussed what hard work and having goals meant to him and to numerous other athletes. Writing down goals and having a plan of action to achieve them was something he suggested. Everyone has goals we are striving for: winning the competition, losing weight and getting fit, working at a hobby regularly, graduating from college, finding a new career, getting a promotion, or raising a family. Indeed, everyone has his or her own "gold medals" to win in life.

However, to win our own gold medal requires paying the price. We need to put the sweatpants on and do the work: run the extra wind sprints at the end of a difficult football practice, make the additional sales call at the end of the day to reach quota, or as a student, put in more study time and participate in the extra credit, or be willing to make the many sacrifices necessary to raise a family. In other words, we need to do the work to win the prize and accomplish our goals.

The third guidepost is about our attitude. Believing we deserve great things reveals an interesting perspective about our attitude. Attitude is a specific way of living your life. Many of us live our life not believing we deserve the best life can offer. Sometimes it is finding the best in life's tough and challenging times that presents the opportunity for us to grow rather than becoming bitter or not improving at all.

Often, when we accomplish all three of the above, we still do not attain our goal. If we have written goals, work hard for our goals, and have a great attitude, yet we don't receive the promotion, win the game, receive a *B* grade versus the *A*, have we failed? Mr. Richards shared many stories of successful athletes who set goals, did the work with the right attitude, and yet did not reach their ultimate goals.

The one I fondly remember is the story of Randy Gardner and Tai Babilonia, United States pair figure skaters. They were five-time U.S. champions and world champions entering the 1980 Olympics. About two weeks before the Olympics, Randy pulled a groin muscle. They kept it a secret and believed it had healed enough to compete. When they entered to skate for their first program in the Olympics, Randy fell performing a jump. The crowd gasped. The television audience and the stadium crowd wondered what had happened to the reigning world champions. He had taken a pain-killing injection, which caused numbness, and he did not have the usual feeling in his injured leg. They could not compete, let alone accomplish their lifelong dream of winning an Olympic gold medal. Why did this occur? Was it chance, destiny, bad luck? Was it a bigger plan from God? Only one person or team gets the gold medal, while all others (including Randy and Tai) fall short. What is to be learned from this?

Reflecting back on Bob's speech, his fundamental message is clear and simple. It is the process, the journey to aspire to our goals, which most vividly defines us. It is not the achievement of the goal, but the hard work and the progress made along the way. It is the person we become in the daring achievement to "go for the gold." Harry Chapin said, "it's got to be the going, not the getting there that is good." As Bob Richards accepted the gold medal around his neck, it took about two minutes for the national anthem to play. That was the end. He achieved his ultimate goal of winning the Olympic Gold Medal. He challenged those of us listening to embrace the joy of that single moment of metaphorically winning our own gold medal. However, more importantly, he said, we need to understand the greater treasure and gratification, in all the work we perform, to try and stand on the podium and win our own gold medal.

We all make tremendous sacrifices in our lives striving for our goals: spending countless hours studying to graduate from high school or college, working long hours finishing a project at work, growing our career over years with complete dedication and understanding the numerous setbacks and disappointments occurring along the way.

Raising children is one of the most meaningful sacrifices many of us make as human beings. We need to be selfless in putting others in front of our needs. My daughter, Cailie, and her husband, Jeff, are new parents and now understand the sacrifices involved in raising a family. Cailie has decided to nurse Luke Michael Ryan. As I discovered with Barbara, nursing a newborn/infant requires complete dedication and selflessness. Regular sleep for parents of a newborn baby is a precious commodity.

It is the process and the journey we must love to continue on in the pursuit of our elusive goals. It is the love of our work and the love of learning that is necessary. These are the components of goals in our own tool kit. Whatever your goals are, it isn't about winning, but striving to win. It is about struggling to do your best, pushing yourself beyond what you mentally and physically believe you can do. Essentially, you win the prize with your attitude and effort. The iconic figure in pro football Mike Ditka says, "failure occurs only when we stop trying."

Let us now explore a deeper understanding of goals. Although setting goals improves performance robustly across various settings, it is a skill one must learn. Setting goals motivates people through their learning and desired accomplishments. Before we discuss the specific types of goals, I believe it is important to consider several aspects to successful goal attainment.

Before setting any goal, take an inventory of why

you want to accomplish this goal. How long will this goal take to achieve? How motivated are you to begin the work? Are you conscientious? A study done by researchers Bipp and Kleingeld found the personality trait of conscientiousness (the capacity for self-control in terms of planning, organization, and task accomplishment) is an important trait for successful goal attainment. What will the end outcome look like? An example might be earning an extra $2,500 from a bonus plan at work. The outcome is receiving the $2,500. But, what will you do with the money? Is it paying for your children's private school, making a donation to your favorite charity, paying down debt on your credit cards, or all of the above? The specific actions and things we do with the money motivate us more than just the outcome of earning an additional $2,500.

Successful goal attainment starts with writing down your goals. Studies on goal-setting adamantly support this written exercise. It triggers something in our brain, gives us ownership and keeps us more accountable.

My recommendation is our goals in the tool kit should be SMART goals:
- **S**pecific, significant
- **M**easurable, meaningful, quantifiable
- **A**chievable, having an action plan to move forward
- **R**ealistic, relevant
- **T**ime-sensitive, thoughtful

An example of a SMART goal is "I will lose five pounds in thirty days." This is specific, measurable, achievable, realistic, and time sensitive (thirty days).

TOOL BOX

FOLLOW EACH STEP IN ORDER

1. Reflect on and write three goals you achieved in high school, college, or your first job.

   a. _____

   b. _____

   c. _____

2. Write three personal and/or career goals for the next twelve months.

   a. _____

   b. _____

   c. _____

   Evaluate whether these are SMART goals. Rewrite them if necessary.

3. Place copies of your written SMART goals where you can see them every day. Maybe on your kitchen table, your phone, car, a mirror in your bathroom.

4. Twice a week, spend fifteen minutes thinking about your goals.

5. Develop a scoring system you can track monthly. This is designed to determine if are you on track or behind in achieving your goals. The system I use is red, yellow, and green. Red is behind on your goal or losing, yellow is no progress since last tracked, and green is meeting your goal or winning.

6. Once a month, assess your scoring system and make adjustments to stay on course for meeting your short term, annual, or longer-term goal.

Everyone should have goals growing up. The most significant goal for me was to graduate from college. Since my parents were not able to assist me financially, I needed to earn my own way. Because I was athletic, I thought this could best be accomplished by earning a baseball or football scholarship. As children, we model behavior of our parents, siblings, and friends as we grow up. But sometimes we learn from our role models to take a different course of action.

My four older siblings had not attended college, yet I learned much from them growing up. I learned from my oldest sister, Christine, the power of perseverance and having a positive attitude in the face of tremendous adversity. My sister Val wanted to work after high school so she started a great job and worked for many years. I saw loyalty and hard work from Val. Eileen was kind and loving. Barbara and I were seventeen when she loaned us her burnt-orange, high-powered Monte Carlo for the weekend of prom. We gratefully returned the car unscathed. Eileen also taught me how to be totally committed and in love. She married her first love. Rich, my oldest brother, finished high school in five years. I can hear Mom telling Ricky, "you are going to finish high school no matter how long it takes." He had persistence and indeed finished high school. I learned that goals are not linear and often there are unforeseen obstacles along the journey.

I wanted to attend college. I envisioned escaping where I grew up in Morton Grove, Illinois. It is a middle-class suburb, not poor but not wealthy. I am not sure where my drive came from. In the end, it does not matter if it was from genetics, God, or doing the opposite of some of my siblings' behavior. Rich is a wonderful human being who taught me how to be a loving father, amazingly involved grandpa, wonderful friend, and a great brother. Yet in his youth in the sixties and seventies, Rich never met a drug he did not try. I guess doing the opposite was my path at the time.

I did everything in my power to be a good student and an athlete who might have a chance for a scholarship. In the winter of 1975, I was invited to visit West Point by an assistant football coach, Mr. Bowman. Barbara and I drove to West Point with her Mom, Eleanor, and stayed at a general's home. The visit started with a thorough physical exam. The following day, we walked with coach Bowman along the Hudson River. He had us visualize General Washington coming up the river during the American Revolutionary war. On this road trip, we visited several other schools. West Point remained a distinct possibility. Yet I would not be allowed to play baseball, and a five-year commitment after graduation gave me pause. When the University of Minnesota offered me a football scholarship, the ability to play baseball, and become an engineer, I eagerly accepted.

For Barbara, one of her life goals was to be accepted into a graduate school program and attain her PhD. In 1983, she began her studies at Loyola University in Chicago. She graduated with our four young children in attendance and received her PhD in January of 1994. It was a day filled with anticipation, wonder, gratitude, and respect for Barbara's dedication for over ten years. My wife had a goal of earning her PhD and she accomplished her goal. Today, I still marvel at the work she put in as a student, Mom, and wife. She was with the kids all day, drove them back and forth to school, played with them, and made dinner for all of us. Then, at night, she worked on her studies and eventually her dissertation. Barbara lacked regular sleep for more than a decade. She truly paid a price and "put the sweat pants on." I am still overwhelmed at the incredible effort and persistence Barbara exemplified in reaching her goal.

Over the years, I have thought numerous times of Bob Richards' fourth guidepost: "allow the possibility we may not achieve our goals." It reminds me of the term "small victories." I have found this Mike Lauesen saying, "small victories," has profoundly impacted my adult life.

Let's imagine a goal of graduating high school in the top 25 percent of the graduating class. If we graduate in the top 33 percent, have we failed? Surely we experienced many small victories in our academics during high school. We may have been more challenged in a few classes then we anticipated, yet we persevered in the semester. Perhaps we achieved a higher grade in a math class than we ever imagined. Balancing academics and activities outside of school are small victories. Possibly we participated in the jazz band and even played a lead role in a musical. Although the extra curricular activities may have compromised our grades, we participated in a well-rounded high school education. Making every effort to reach our goal and enjoying small victories along the way is what is important.

Baseball is a game of small victories. It is a nuanced and complicated game. You may go hitless during the game, yet make two stellar defensive plays that were keys to a victory. A pitcher did not have his best stuff, yet kept the game close for seven innings, a small victory for the pitcher, but a win for the team. Battling a *strikeout pitcher* for a base on balls is a small victory.

Often there are many steps to achieving a goal. When I entered the University of Minnesota, my goal was to graduate with an engineering degree. The timeframe is generally four or more years to graduate from college.

I eventually graduated with an accounting degree. The milestones I needed for the degree were similar to engineering. It was the same number of credit hours and similar time spent studying. But it was a different degree. My journey was bumpy and rocky throughout the first two years of college. I navigated through three different colleges at the University of Minnesota. The Engineering school was first, then the College of Liberal Arts, and finally the Business School. I had many small victories along the way. Getting *A*s in my financial and managerial accounting classes set me on the road to obtaining a bachelor of science in accounting. I celebrated those *A*s.

Rewarding ourselves for the small victories is critical to keeping us motivated and having a positive attitude. For a special occasion, Mom and Dad used to reward themselves and celebrate by going out to dinner. This happened very infrequently; it made an indelible impression on me. What ways do you reward yourself for the small victories in your life? Do you treat yourself to a day off work, go to a spa and relax, see a movie, or open that collectible bottle of wine? Whatever you do in rewarding yourself for the valiant effort in working toward your goals, make it a first-class celebration.

From all aspects of our lives, coaches, mentors, trusted advisors, parents, siblings, teachers, coaches in sports and activities, bosses at work, clergy, and even the individual we meet once can have a lasting impact. We need all of them to enable us to stay focused, motivated, and inspired in striving to attain our goals.

My countless mentors and coaches include my parents, siblings, kids, wife, college baseball coach, Bob Richards, and many friends and business colleagues. Up until age fourteen, Dad was my pitching coach for baseball. I then had other high school coaches. An amazing athlete himself, Al Eck was my high school football coach. He taught me how to have fun in football. In addition, I was able to learn about finding balance in life. Spending time with Al outside of the gridiron, I was lucky to observe him not only as a football coach but as a father, husband, and know him as a friend. In college, my baseball coach, George Thomas, was a wonderful mentor for baseball and life. I learned focus, love of practice, and not taking life and baseball too seriously. I would not have received a scholarship, college degree, and developed my own philosophy of sports without coaches like Al, George, and other mentors along the way.

When I started my own company, I had a dream to grow revenues up to twenty-five million dollars. The dream and goal were eventually fulfilled, but it was never about the revenue. It was about building something bigger than me and enjoying the ride along the way with a team of dedicated peers. We could never have built a successful small business without the aid of mentors and coaches. I had a personal and business coach named Jim Geimer. For sixteen years, Jim guided, questioned, and provided insight. Can you imagine his dedication, love, and often his patience with me? I was very fortunate to have Jim as a business coach. My business group, in which I participated with Jim, provided direction, inspiration, and practical tools to assist me in my life's work. Starting my current work as a Chair for Vistage International, Steve Larrick, an accomplished and successful Vistage chair, coached me for one year.

Coaches hold us accountable to our goals. Michael Jordan, arguably the greatest basketball player, had many coaches to be accountable to in his life. He continued to master his craft with nutrition coaches, fitness coaches, shooting coaches, and a head basketball coach, Phil Jackson, who was called a Zen Master. In David Halberstam's book about Michael Jordan, *Playing for Keeps*, he discusses the psyche of Michael Jordan. Jordan worked methodically with his trainers and nutritionist over four years, gaining five pounds per year so it would not negatively impact his shooting ability. That is crazy dedication.

Trust is an important aspect of the relationship we have with our mentors and coaches. Trust is the foundation of healthy relationships. In a trusting relationship, our coaches encourage and challenge us without judgment. These trusting relationships assist us to be more committed and invested in our goals. This feedback from our coaches and mentors is the foundational cornerstone of successful goal attainment.

Who are your coaches and mentors? Do you need a coach or mentor now to begin your goal setting?

TOOL BOX

Decide who your mentors or coaches will be to assist you in accomplishing your goals. Write down who they will be.

_____

_____

_____

_____

_____

_____

_____

_____

With paying attention as our foundational piece, we now have utilizing goals as our second tool. Bob Richards reminds us to write our goals, work hard for them with the right attitude, and allow the possibility we will not achieve all our lifelong dreams and goals. Lessons learned in goal-setting are to enjoy the process and travel on the journey with clarity and joy while we strive for our goals. To achieve our SMART goals, we need to be motivated, conscientious, and persevere.

What are *your* current goals for the next twelve months you articulated on the SMART goal worksheet? To accomplish our goals, we have to be cognizant of small victories and celebrate them along the way. Coaches and mentors assist us in our goal attainment by keeping us accountable in a caring and trusting manner.

Who are *your* coaches and mentors? If we pay attention to our written goals and joyfully work toward them, we can realize more than we imagine.

While you are awake and in your peaceful, quiet place, imagine what it feels like to accomplish your goals and even achieve your wildest dreams. Do the necessary work and enjoy the journey.

The next addition to our tool kit is "starting simply."

CHAPTER FIVE

Start Simply

We have added two tools to our kit. *Pay Attention,* similar to my Dad's blueprint, is the substructure of our tools. The second tool, *Utilize Goals,* resembles a level providing direction and guideposts for the journey of our life. With any craftsman, a hammer is basic and necessary. Our next tool, *Start Simply,* is the hammer in our toolbox. Correspondingly, start simply is vital to uncover our life purpose and to get off the treadmill of life. The dictionary defines "simply" as:

1. In a simple manner; clearly and easily

2. Plainly; unaffectedly

3. Sincerely; artlessly: to speak simply as a child

4. Merely; only: It is simply a cold

5. Unwisely; foolishly: If you behave simply toward him, you're bound to be betrayed

6. Wholly; absolutely: simply irresistible

Of the six definitions, the first is the best for our discussion. A good example of starting simply is training for a marathon. This can involve many months or even years. If we attempt to run a marathon without being in running shape, we would fail. Starting simply is analogous to the training you begin to complete a marathon. Your first race should be a 5K or 10K. *Start Simply* by running or walking short distances a few times a week. Next, run three to four times a week, gradually working up to longer distances and difficulties. Peaking for the race in twelve weeks, you accomplish your first goal. You started simply. Moving on to running a half-marathon is the next step to completing a full marathon. Running distances will be longer and more frequent. Completing a half-marathon is a notable step in attaining your goal of running a marathon. Starting simply is starting where we are today and achieving small victories (races) along the way to the end goal of a full marathon.

Let's divide *Start Simply* into several categories called the "Wheel of Life." Some of these categories are:

1. Family

2. Relationships

3. Spirituality

4. Career

5. Finances

6. Travel

7. Health: physical, mental, emotional

8. Leisure, relaxation

These are listed in no particular order. You can add, change, or subtract from this list. This is your *life! Start Simply*, get off the treadmill, and begin a race to live a more significant and fulfilling life.

How many hours are in a week? There are 168 hours in a week. This does not change. We consistently have 168 hours per week to sleep, work, relax, travel, read, meditate, exercise, etc. How much time do you spend in each category? Do you spend as much time with your family as your career? How many hours per week do you spend in your relationships?

Do you travel often? How many hours do you focus on your health? What about leisure and relaxing time?

Working forty hours at a specific job or running our households, then adding an average commute time, this comes to approximately fifty to fifty-five hours per week. We sleep around forty-five to fifty-five hours per week. This leaves us over sixty hours per week. What do you do with the sixty hours?

I believe where you spend your free time tells you much about yourself. I define "free time" as a choice we make and have the most influence over: the sixty hours. Reflect where your time is spent in an average week. When you have free time, what do you do? Read, watch a movie, attend family activities, pray?

I love to read. Mom taught me this. Although I read the newspaper and a few magazines, books are my passion. Historical fiction, nonfiction, inspirational stories, and books on health are my preferred topics. Although I do other things in my free time, reading provides the most joy and pleasure and brings me to my peaceful, quiet place regularly.

As you pay attention, you can begin to focus on what is most important to you in your free time. It could be walks in your neighborhood, working out, watching movies, church or civic duties, playing an instrument, relaxing with family and friends, or a combination of all. Remember, we only have 168 hours in one week and approximately sixty hours of free time.

TOOL BOX

LIFE CATEGORIES AND PRIORITIES

1. Review the Life Categories/Wheel of Life; feel free to add your own categories, modify, or use what I provided.

2. Write the approximate time you currently spend in each category or grouping.

   Family _____

   Relationships _____

   Spirituality _____

   Career _____

Finances _____

Travel _____

Health: physical, mental, emotional _____

Leisure, relaxation _____

3. Write your smart goal for number of hours in each section or category.

Family _____

Relationships _____

Spirituality _____

Career _____

Finances _____

Travel _____

Health: physical, mental, emotional _____

Leisure, relaxation _____

4. Fill in the number of hours you have free time.

_____

_____

_____

_____

5. List what you *want* to do with your free time.

_____

_____

_____

_____

6. Pay attention to what you currently do versus what you *want* to do in your "spare time."

7. Create a SMART goal for your own "sixty hours" of time outside of work, commuting, and sleeping. *Start Simply,* with the first line of your smart goal: "I will spend ___ hours per week doing the following...."

_____

_____

_____

_____

8. Determine who your coach or coaches will be. Meet with your coach at least monthly to assist you in accomplishing your goals.

Realizing this exercise utilizing SMART goals may change over time throughout different phases of our life; the purpose is to get started simply. A young adult may spend more time with relationships and school. If we are raising a family, we might have more time with our children. A significant amount of time for grandparents may be spent on travel, grandchildren, and leisure time. When we begin our careers, we might focus a meaningful amount of time building our experience and credentials to further our careers.

We often spend time on the urgent—what we feel needs to be done in the moment. Urgent does not imply it is important. Doing the above exercise allows us to think and focus on what is most significant in our life. The Wheel of Life provides a fresh look with our families, careers, spiritual lives, friends, and many others.

Relationships are important in my life. Before my kids entered high school, I scheduled time in the calendar to make sure I spent one-on-one time with each of them. During the normal week with four children, going to different schools, involved with sports and activities, it was chaotic. One-on-one time with my kids may have been the Daddy-Daughter dance, a movie, playing catch, coaching, or reading. It was sometimes as simple as having lunch or dinner together.

I still spend special time with my kids. My goal is to take a one-week vacation with them before they turn thirty. At the time of writing this book, I have been blessed to spend a glorious week with my three oldest adult children, Conor, Erin, and Cailie. Realizing how privileged I am to take a vacation with each of my children, I do not ever take this time, leisure, and pleasure for granted. Fortunately for me, my children each want to spend time with dear old Dad.

Taylor, our youngest, will be next. Taylor suggested we travel to Iceland for our trip together. She has investigated Iceland thoroughly. I must admit having anxiety with some of the excursions we can consider traveling in Iceland. Some of the many adventures are hiking ice caves and glaciers, viewing the northern lights, and exploring a volcano referred to in Jules Verne's book *A Journey to the Center of the Earth*. We hope to take a vacation together sometime in the next few years.

Sedona and the Grand Canyon was an inspiring experience for Erin and me a few years ago. Erin is my oldest daughter and is an old soul. As a toddler, she was blessed with the gift of wisdom, and this continues today. Her strength, courage, and passion for life are enviable to all who know her. Social justice through urban education is Erin's calling.

The Sedona vicinity is known for the unusual colors of the sandstone. These unique colors are only found in this area. We hiked through this solitary geological area and were awed by the majestic red and orange colors. When we departed, I was excited to see the Grand Canyon, yet I did not believe the sights could be more wildly impressive than the pictures so often reproduced. Although I had never visited either area, the Grand Canyon is a visual spectacle beyond the imagination. It is 277 miles long, up to eighteen miles wide, deeper than a mile, and formed by the Colorado River millions of years ago. Erin had the wisdom to pick a place as old and stunning as the Grand Canyon. We continued hiking. Resting often on the climbs up, we turned in circles, absorbing all the entire canyon offered. On the last day, we rented bikes. As we approached each corner, the views were even more monumental. The varying colors of the mile-deep creviced formations were grandiose. The majestic beauty is unsurpassed. It needs to be seen to be believed. Although the awesome sights were incomparable, the quiet alone-time spent together with my daughter was most precious. Our holiday finished in Las Vegas, where Erin treated me to a scrumptious dinner with breathtaking views from our table.

Cycling has become a passion and brings me into the zone regularly. When Cailie suggested we bike Oregon for our special vacation, I sprinted to take the opportunity. Cailie has been unusually blessed with brute strength since she was two years old. She is articulate and self-confidant. If Cailie sets her mind to something, consider it accomplished. Her physical fitness was exemplified on our daily rides.

We utilized Backroads, a travel company specifically renowned for cycling. They assisted us daily with our snacks, route maps, and dinners over the six days of our journey. The highlight of the trip was biking up Crater Lake and riding around the crater. It was formed over 7,000 years ago by a collapsed volcano. Nearly 2,000 feet deep, it is the deepest lake in America. The blue chilling waters glistened as the sun came over the crater throughout the day. Although Cailie was seventeen weeks pregnant, she climbed the nearly 8,000-foot elevation to the top. Arriving at the lodge, we showered and relaxed around a fire and had a quiet dinner overlooking the crater. The other cyclists on the trip marveled at her attitude and ability to bike uphill climbs while pregnant. She was the rock star of the cycling group. We then had a few relaxing days in Seattle and enjoyed each other's company out of the bike saddle.

Conor and I went to the Grand Tetons a few summers ago and stayed in beautiful Jackson, Wyoming. Our intention was to spend time together and hike the majestic Tetons. Conor is currently working on his PhD in art history. He is not only extremely bright, but also very athletic. The park rangers' guide labeled our first hike very difficult and strenuous. Climbing uphill for three hours, periodically losing our breath, was a steep challenge. I wanted to turn around several times. Conor encouraged me to stay the course. When we reached the snowy peak at 10,500 feet, we relaxed and absorbed the natural beauty. Glistening pools of picturesque blue waters enchanted us. Panoramic sights of the surrounding landscape inspired us and burned brilliant memories into our souls. It was a God moment.

Extremely tired, yet proud of reaching the top of the mountain, we rested, ate our scrumptious snacks and drank ice-cold water. In this glorious moment in time, the indescribable thirst and hunger in our stomachs, minds, and souls were quenched. Descending, we quickly realized it was going to be significantly faster on the return down the wooded, rocky terrain than the struggle up. It took only two hours to reach our starting point.

Near the end of our hike, we had a harrowing

experience. As we neared the final 1000 meters of our hike, Conor and I encountered a grizzly bear approximately seventy-five feet from our path. According to the park rangers' hiking guide, the last thing you were supposed to do was to be quiet around a bear. We, however, being both naïve and unaware, were stunned and scared into silence. The intimidating bear was in a grassy area and was voraciously eating, making eye contact several unsettling times. We slowly crept behind a tree with trepidation, anxiety, and amazement. The hiking manual suggests you cannot out run a bear, and should not attempt to do so. Throwing caution to the wind, we ran as fast as we could, sprinting for five minutes, never looking back. Although Conor could easily outrun me, he honored my ability and stayed beside me in my full sprint. It was the fastest I had run since college. It was exhilarating. Arriving at our car safely, we recovered for several minutes. Later, we enjoyed a fabulous dinner and reflected on the memorable day and what we had accomplished and experienced together as father and son.

We were definitely *good tired* (more on this in the last chapter). Starting the day simply to take a hike, we experienced more than we ever could have imagined. The hike is one of my fondest memories with Conor.

The marvelous and beautiful places we visited are no match for the exceptional time together with each of my kids. Each trip was out of the ordinary. We were together for twenty-four hours each day in incomparable natural settings. God and nature created these spectacular sights. Yet Barbara and I, with the help of God, created these four extraordinary human beings. I am enormously grateful for the opportunity.

What is to be learned from this? Spend time on what is important to you. Be with the people you love when possible. We never get back the time we do not spend with our families and friends. Time passes much too quickly. Benjamin Franklin said, "lost time is never found again." I learned this lesson with my wife Barbara.

While my wife was in graduate school, and I had started my company, Nicoat, a few years earlier, I read a book called *Keeping Your Family Together When the World is Falling Apart,* by Kevin Lehman. A reluctant lesson learned from Dr. Lehman's book was to put your marriage first or equal to your family. At the time I read this book, we had four children nine years old and younger. Barbara was in the middle of writing her PhD dissertation. We were living on credit cards and scrambling financially to get the business profitable. It was overwhelming, stressful, and exhausting for our family.

After reading this book, my response to Barbara was, "This author is nuts; how can we place our marriage first?"

She wholeheartedly agreed, moaning, "I haven't even finished my dissertation." Barbara continued, "I want to be involved in the kids' schools and programs while they are young."

Nodding my head, I said, "We haven't turned the corner at Nicoat and are deeply involved in our kids' sports, activities, and church."

We wondered aloud, "How can our marriage be our focus with all the other facets of our lives pulling us in different directions?"

As we thought about it over the years, the author was correct. Our kids grew up. Barbara graduated with her PhD, and Nicoat eventually thrived. The author was suggesting we pay attention and focus on our marriage *as well as* our families and other important facets of life.

Eventually, we started our own dates together while our kids were relatively young. Taylor, our youngest child, was three when we planned our first trip without the kids.

With amazing clarity, I remember the trip to the Bay Area. As a frequent flyer with United, Barbara and I rode in the comfort of first class. We ordered Bloody Marys immediately as we looked at one another, giggling with anticipation and excitement of the journey ahead. Upon arrival, we rented a car and checked into a luxurious hotel. The bathroom seemed like a photo from architectural digest. As Barbara soaked in the oversized tub, we opened a bottle of red wine and reveled in the moment. A business conference in San Francisco was the catalyst for our first trip together since Conor had been born ten years prior. Spending three unforgettable nights in San Francisco, the conference was an afterthought. Visiting with my best friend, Barbara was exceptional. Napa Valley exceeded all of our expectations; the beauty and charm was not lost on this newly reacquainted couple. For the first time, Barbara was able to shop at Nordstrom without kids. Unbeknownst to me, this set a dangerous precedent in the years to come. Nordstrom became my wife's favorite store in Chicago and it continues to be today! We had three quiet dinners together. I emphasize *quiet*. As many of you surely know, when traveling with the kids, eating out was an adventure in dining. It was a momentous weekend and started simply by arranging the travel. From that trip forward, we focused on our marriage as much as our careers and family.

The time we spend with our loved ones is precious. When we make a choice not to spend time in loving relationships, we need to realize we will never get that time back. Start where you are today. Begin a new chapter prioritizing your time where you feel is the most important category for you in the Wheel of Life.

Baseball is a game of life, and a "simple" game. Or is it? Admittedly, I am biased, as baseball is my favorite sport. I played at a high level and love it. It is more than a sport for me. Having learned some of the most important things in life from baseball, it is in my core being. Here are a few life examples that I relate well to.

If you have a batting average of .300, you are considered

to be very successful. This means you made a base hit thirty out of 100 at-bats. In reality, you failed to achieve a base hit seventy out of 100 times. How is that successful? Baseball developed and trained me to cope well with the ups-and-downs of life. You can strike out three times in your first three at bats, then come up to bat in the last inning and get a base hit or home run to win the game. You hit .250 (batting average: one out of four) for the game (not a very good batting average), but you were the hero with the game-winning hit.

Yet in one game a life can happen. Each pitch is like every minute, hour, day of our lives. In baseball, you have to pay attention every inning and every pitch. Paying attention is the most important tool in baseball. A fielder must be ready to field the ball on every pitch. The pitcher and catcher have to concentrate on each pitch, the count, and the hitter's tendencies. In preparing to hit in your inning of play, each player needs to study the tendency of the pitcher and fielders before they come up to bat. In today's world of video and statistics, all players study different information before games.

There is no time off during a game for the manager of each team. The manager is a strategist, mentor, student, cheerleader, psychologist, and a disciplinarian. He (or she) has to pay attention not only during playable innings, but also in between the innings. Managers have a robust coaching staff whose focal point is preparation before and during a game to gain an edge to win more games than you lose. Is this more complicated than the simple game I mentioned earlier?

When you start playing baseball as a small child, you have very few skills. You have to *Start Simply*. I played catch with my dad for countless hours. At age five, I couldn't throw or catch very well, let alone hit a pitched ball. In college, I honed my skills as an outfielder and line-drive hitter. Countless hours were spent practicing fly balls, doing toss hit (hitting the baseball into a net with someone throwing a short distance to you), and hitting in batting practice. The mental and physical preparation at the college level is significantly more complex than in little league. Likewise, the preparation at the professional level is far beyond college. Wherever you are in your baseball career, you are always starting simply. Simple things in baseball make us better and win more games.

Baseball has parallels to our life and career. As with Bob Richards' second guidepost, we have to pay our dues. We have to pay the price to accomplish anything worthwhile in life. When we *Start Simply*, we begin each day starting over. This might be a fresh new start in a baseball game, or each day at home, work, with our families, friends, and in all other interests in life. Make a choice to *Start Simply* in each facet of your Wheel of Life. It is simple. Work hard and do the right thing.

When we *Start Simply*, it brings humility to improve daily in all areas of life. The knowledge and skills we acquire often create an illusion in our minds. I like to say we can become "puffed up." We think we have arrived or made it—believing we have mastered our craft, reached the pinnacle of our career, sport, or educational level. Getting caught up in our successes, do we forget where we started? Starting simply opens up the possibility to continue to learn, gain insights, and attempt to master our own life wheel. We may never master different aspects of our life, but it is fun trying.

Einstein first developed the special theory of relativity in 1905, and then in 1915 developed his general theory of relativity. He continued to work as a physicist until his death in 1955. Physics, science, and space would be different today if Albert Einstein stopped his research after 1905. Yet, did he ever master physics?

Reminding ourselves how we started our education, careers, and spiritual journeys, keeps us grounded to *Start Simply* in our wheel of life.

Life is beautiful and simple. We make it more complicated than it is. Think back to the first book you read. What about the first game you competed in? Could you go back to high school today and be a better student? What was your first full-time job, and how much was your paycheck?

We all attended first grade. Be a first-grader in your mind. If you have not read a book to a first-grader, give it a try. It provides a lens to our past. Have you played soccer or tag with a first grader? It is worthwhile playing with them. We are reminded of the uncomplicated, simple joy of starting simply doing an activity.

A mantra for our children when they were young was, "be good, be respectful, make us proud, be a Lauesen". We repeated this phrase so often, they eventually tired of Barbara and I reciting it. Yet, as parents, being good and being respectful was simple. If you did both of those, you made us proud as parents. This was a mantra for starting simply that our kids appreciate more as adults.

We have 168 hours in every week. This is a constant today, tomorrow, and for the rest of our lives. Review the Tool worksheet earlier in this chapter titled "Life Categories." Do you want to make any additions and/ or changes to your categories and the time you *want* to spend in each group? The next chapter, Reflect Daily, will assist you in this reevaluation of your life wheel.

Starting simply is the hammer in our toolbox. It is the most primary of our tools. Dad would not be able to start, let alone finish, his job assignments without his hammer. When we utilize starting simply, it complements all our other tools and is necessary to escape the race to nowhere. Once you internalize *Start Simply*, all your tools become integrated into your own life philosophy.

Francis of Assisi said, "Start by doing what's necessary; then do what's possible; and suddenly you are doing the impossible." What an amazing, thoughtful, insightful description of starting simply.

Let us move on to our fourth tool: *Reflect Daily*.

CHAPTER SIX

Reflect Daily

As we add instruments to our tool kit they sharpen our ability to live an intentional life of purpose. Last chapter, we added *Start Simply* as the hammer in our tool kit. Now our kit includes three tools: *Pay Attention* (blueprint); *Utilize Goals* (level); and *Start Simply* (hammer).

Dad used a magnifying glass, which is a similar tool to a microscope. *Reflect Daily* is our fourth tool and the microscope of our life.

The dictionary defines "reflect" as:

1. To be turned or cast back, as light.

2. To cast back light, heat, etc.

3. To think, ponder, or meditate: to reflect on one's virtues and faults.

This one resonates for me: "To think, ponder, or meditate: to reflect on one's virtues and faults." As we reflect daily, we see the world through a magnificent optical lens as we gaze inwardly, beyond the exterior of our physical being.

Do you remember your high school science class and how much fun it was learning how to maneuver a microscope? A microscope is an optical instrument with a magnifying lens or a combination of lenses for inspecting objects too small to be seen distinctly and in detail by the unaided eye. A microscope is an apparatus designed to view details in life we do not see in our normal field of vision. Unlike a mirror, which reflects an image we place in front of it including our self, a microscope penetrates the surface. We see deeper with more significance than just the apparent.

With our busy lives, how will we accomplish this every day? Let's explore the groundwork through which we can reflect daily and what daily reflection will do to help us get off the treadmill. There are many ways to reach this.

Here are a few:

1. Gratefulness
2. Breathing
3. Meditation
4. Rituals
5. Thin places

It is necessary to understand these tools and techniques to begin your own daily reflection. They have aided me, yet I need constant reminders and structure to accomplish a daily reflection. Reflecting every day provides numerous benefits. Most notable are learning, finding new perspectives, and improving each and every day. Stress can be reduced, and we can be rejuvenated. And it helps us get off the treadmill.

Gratefulness

Gratefulness is our first technique to *Reflect Daily*. Reminders of how grateful we should be and the blessings in our life surround us every day. The daunting challenge is seeing and experiencing these blessings. When we regularly count our blessings, it allows us to be appreciative every day. When we *Pay Attention*, reminders to be grateful are around us every minute, hour, and day. We need to constantly seek them because it allows us to reflect daily.

REFLECT DAILY—GRATEFULNESS

Follow each step, in order.

1. List what you are grateful for.

   The following may help you get started: Reading, working out, good health, growing up with freedoms in America, sleep, family, friends, mentors, vacations, money, giving to charities, grocery stores, medical care, and regular work. Make sure you include basic needs such as shelter, food, water, walking, seeing, and hearing. Your list should provide a multitude of things to be grateful for.

_____

_____

_____

_____

_____

_____

_____

_____

_____

_____

_____

_____

_____

_____

_____

_____

_____

2. For one week, add to your list each morning.

Day 1:_____

Day 2:_____

Day 3:_____

Day 4:_____

Day 5:_____

Day 6:_____

Day 7:_____

3. Review the list daily.

I am appreciative on cold days in Chicago for heat in our home and cars. I think about the many folks who struggle to pay their heating bills or even have a warm home. We thankfully use our fireplace for the smell, sounds, beauty, and warmth, but not to heat our home. On warm humid summer days, I am thankful for air conditioning. Barbara and I consider ourselves lucky as we can comfortably afford to pay the electric bill for the air conditioning during the summer months.

My father could not afford a new car until I was in college. His cars always needed repairs and were often in the shop. Dad had them "Band-Aid-ed" together to keep them running. Often the loudest cars on the road due to muffler problems, they had dents, rust, and probably belonged in the junkyard. As a result, I was often embarrassed driving in these "junkers." Purchasing my first new car after college, I thought a lot about my dad: how hard he worked to eventually purchase a new Chevy Caprice Classic with all the options. Dad was proud and grateful to finally own a new car. I shared in his pride as I placed a University of Minnesota sticker on the rear window. Driving a luxury car for several years, I am always thankful for having the resources to own such a fine automobile. Realizing a large percentage of the world population does not have the financial resources to own a luxury auto, let alone a car, I try very hard to not take this for granted.

Erin and Cailie both worked as teachers for an organization called Teach for America. Here is the mission: "Our mission is to enlist, develop, and mobilize as many as possible of our nation's most promising future leaders to grow and strengthen the movement for educational equity and excellence." Eventually leaving the classrooms, they are now on staff in the Chicago office of Teach for America. Erin and Cailie assist teachers in their first few years of teaching to help them become high-performing teachers and bridge the education gap in impoverished areas.

Cailie stays in touch with preschool kids she taught several years ago. She is thankful she can be in contact with these children and their parents are delighted a teacher continues to care. Understanding how privileged she was growing up in an affluent suburb of Chicago, Cailie decided to make a difference in teaching with Teach for America. As a father, I was not aware of this education and opportunity gap until Erin and Cailie worked as teachers and mentors at Teach for America.

I grew up in a middle-class town with good schools and very few people of color. Morton Grove, my hometown, is the opposite of the communities Erin and Cailie work with. Safety was never a concern in my neighborhood. Children living in low-income areas experience gunshots and killings much too often. I grew up with two loving parents and a family of siblings from the same biological parents. This is not commonplace in the impoverished areas of Chicago. My high school had a very high graduation rate and it was common for kids to attend and graduate college. In most major cities like Chicago, graduation rates in public high schools are below fifty percent. Attending college is significantly less common. I reflect how fortunate and beholden I am, as a white male, to grow up in a middle-class suburb. Having a traditional family, receiving an excellent public school education through high school, I had more privilege than most children growing up in the urban centers of the United States.

Erin coaches middle-school boys' basketball. She coaches many of the kids she taught when they were in second grade. The basketball players have been to our home many times over the past years. Thinking about middle-school and high-school kids "invading" my quiet space, I often groaned the question to Barbara: "Do they have to come again?" Inevitably, I have an "aha" moment during their visit and am able to reflect on all the blessings in my life and what we can share with the kids.

The children visiting our home do not live in safe neighborhoods. They do not own bikes, let alone ride them around their neighborhoods. Bike riding has taken on new meaning in the Lauesen home. It does not matter how cold or miserable the weather is; the kids want to ride bikes. They take turns riding our "old" bikes around our upper-class suburb of Glenview. Seeing the jubilant freedom and joy is a wonderful and precious feeling they cannot experience near their homes. Erin and Cailie have "stretched" our entire family and me by doing great work for kids at risk.

Recently Barbara drove some of the kids home after a basketball game. She needed gas in her car. One of the kids asked her, "Are you filling up the car?" Think about that question. When was the last time you were not able to fill up your vehicle because of financial reasons? The last time for me was during college. Perhaps filling up the car is not a common occurrence in these kid's lives. I am grateful for not worrying about the cost of filling up.

After basketball games, Erin drives some of the kids home. One Saturday evening a tournament game ended after 9:00 p.m. The last teammate she dropped off found no one home. Erin called the parents, but could not reach them. She had to make a quick decision. Do I drop the child off late at night with no one home or do something else? Erin drove this young boy more than twenty miles to our home in Glenview to spend the night. Why? Erin was afraid to leave the child home without an adult in a dangerous neighborhood. When was the last time you worried about the dangers surrounding the location of your home?

Gratefulness presents itself with every experience we encounter if we *Pay Attention*. Thankfulness is an attitude and a state of mind.

Freshman year at University of Minnesota, I experienced something remarkable. Our football team was running wind sprints at the end of practice. Having trained all summer, I was well conditioned, yet was not prepared for this epiphany. One of our coaches, Mr. McGovern, frowned at all of us in the end zone as we were trying to get our wind. He despairingly said, "Look at the fellow running around the track. What would he give to feel the way you're feeling right now?" It was a young student with a significant disability, laboriously limping around the track next to our practice field. I questioned how I could ever again feel sorry for the fatigue from running fast. I had never given a thought to my innate physical capabilities to run easily. Upon reflection, I was very fortunate to be an athlete with complete physical health.

It was a defining moment for me. When I think about the end zone, wind sprints, and the young student, I am intentionally grateful to walk and run without a problem. Telling the story reminds me of how fortunate and grateful I am physically and this allows me to reflect daily.

How often do we see the person running around the track (without the physical capabilities we are blessed with) and think how charmed we are to have fatigue when we are running or working out? We all have encounters with folks who need a wheelchair for mobility. It is an opportunity to say hello to the stranger with disabilities and reflect on the blessing of physical health.

My father-in-law, John, suffered from depression many years of his life. We worked together for several years. Many days, it was a struggle for John to get to work. Although I have not suffered with depression in my life, many of us know a family member, friend, or colleague who has suffered this debilitating mental health issue. We may not feel the pain, yet we can sympathize with the ongoing struggle of performing simple, everyday tasks that many experience with mental health challenges. We have a choice to be mindful and sensitive of their circumstances and grateful for our mental health.

There are multiple messages and moments every day in our life to say grace, be grateful, and acknowledge our blessings. It is important to consistently seek them out. *Pay Attention*, get off the treadmill, and be grateful every day.

Breathing

Our second technique for daily reflection is breathing. It is necessary for life. It is our birthright. We cannot live without breathing in oxygen and exhaling carbon dioxide. Watching my infant grandson, Luke, breathe is joyous. Babies are belly breathers. We lose this as we age. Breathing is a rhythm of life with infants. Learning is heightened when we pay attention to babies and their breath. It is inherent beauty without thought. Babies breathe, cry, and smile naturally. When we become more aware of our breathing, we gain access outside of conscious awareness and tap into our autonomic nervous system.

TOOL BOX

REFLECT DAILY—BREATH

Follow each step, in order.

1. Be in a quiet place, sit, and relax.

2. Close your eyes.

3. Take three deep breaths. Inhaling, breathe through your nose into your belly and let the air fill up your lungs. On the exhale (through your nose or mouth), let your body round forward a little as the air empties out of you and gently squeeze your abdomen at the end of the exhale.

4. Pay attention to your body and how it feels. Relax each limb.

5. Repeat this activity three to four times a day for a month. It may become a habit.

In our fast-paced society, days can be filled with continual stress-inducers. This stress leads to our bodies living on high alert, commonly known as fight-or-flight response mode. Breathing is one method to let the stress go and reflect on our breath for minutes at a time. This can recalibrate us into an alert, calm state of being. As you regularly practice intentional breathing, you can begin to reflect daily on how this simple technique slowly exits us off the treadmill and the race to nowhere.

Meditation

A few years ago, Barbara and I attended a six-week meditation workshop. According to the dictionary, meditation is defined as continued or extended thought; reflection; contemplation.

We attended class one day a week for ninety minutes. Our goals were to be more mindful in daily life and learn to meditate. Our teacher learned from a yogi in India. She was kind, experienced, grounded, and paid attention. After each class, there were techniques and practices we worked on daily until the next class. Gradually increasing daily meditation time was a goal for all participants.

The second week, we were expected to meditate daily for five minutes. Each week we learned about the art and science of meditation and shared what we learned. During our last class, we reported our progress.

I shared with the class that these daily meditations

were difficult, unsettling, challenging, and yet rewarding. Although I was up to twenty minutes of daily meditation, I was not confident I'd continue the practice. It was difficult to quiet my mind, breathe, and practice the various techniques. As much as I would like to meditate, I don't. I am hopeful to make it a priority in the future.

Barbara told our teacher with a quivering, emotional voice she could not meditate for ten minutes, let alone twenty. My wife is very loving. She is unequivocally sincere, passionate, and vulnerable; Barbara is a high-energy human being who emanates positivity. She prefers hugs to handshakes, smiles to frowns, and giving versus receiving.

A twenty-minute meditation was like swimming the English Channel for her. Our teacher was not on the treadmill. She clearly paid attention to my wife and actively listened to her struggles. She asked Barbara if she could meditate twenty times a day, for a minute each. *Start Simply*, our tool from last chapter, was her perspective. What a brilliant suggestion! We smiled at one another and let out a sigh of relief. Barbara's nightly "tubby time" is her meditation and daily reflection. It is a grouping of several one-minute intervals. Getting out of the tub, her ritual continues with applying all her various creams to her face and body. Her creams are the three *R*s of creams: repair, restore, and rejuvenate. While she applies her creams, she is doing her daily reflection. This is a ritual Barbara has practiced for years. Meditation provides a means to *Reflect Daily*.

Have you thought of taking a class or reading a book on meditation? Hopefully you will be inspired to *Start Simply* with registering for a class at a yoga studio or elsewhere.

Rituals

The fourth method for *Reflecting Daily* is rituals. Most world religions have a daily or weekly service. Sunday worship at our church is a regular ritual for Barbara and me. One hour of worship provides us a means to focus on the worship experience, centers our minds on something larger than day-to-day responsibilities of life, and provides a place to reflect on all our blessings in life.

The discipline of attending a service daily or weekly allows reflection and meditation. Holy days in various religions are a means to practice rituals of daily reminders. Ramadan in the Muslim faith includes fasting daily. Jews' yearly atonement for sins is Yom Kippur. Many Christian denominations utilize Lent as a time of sacrifice, repentance, and reflection.

Physical activity can serve as a ritual to think and reflect. Walking clears our mind and helps us become centered and grounded. Walking can be accomplished easily outdoors or on a real treadmill. As mentioned, cycling clears my mind and instills a sense of peace, gratefulness, and a physical challenge all at the same time. What physical activity can you perform to reflect every day? What other rituals do you participate in daily and/or weekly that may bring you to a peaceful reflection?

Incorporating daily reminders creates healthy rituals allowing us to reflect. For many folks, it is a daily reading. This might be a religious book, a book of wisdom such as the "big book" from Alcoholics Anonymous, or a daily quote or message from a particular website or digital app or book. A diary or journal is a simple means to write your thoughts for the day. All these examples are opportunities to create a discipline of reflecting each day.

What activity do you perform every day without exception? It might be something as simple as drinking water, cooking, eating, sleeping, showering or bathing, brushing your teeth, walking, driving, taking public transportation, journaling, or working. Think of your daily activities and pick one. Could this be your own activity or ritual each day to reflect? Remember to mindfully breathe during your activity/ritual.

Thin Places

I last want to consider a technique for reflecting daily: *thin places* is a concept that Marcus Borg, emeritus professor of religion and culture at Oregon State University, developed. Borg writes about *thin places* in his book, *The Heart of Christianity, Rediscovering a Life of Faith*. Here is his definition: *A thin place is where your heart is opened and a veil is lifted between earth and the divine.*

We all experience thin places. It may be described in

different words or terms such as "God moments." Thin places allow us to experience a deeper and profound reflection, which often cannot be articulated.

How and where do these occur? Thin places materialize in nature, wilderness, through music, sounds, breathing, meditation, spiritual experiences, religious services, ordinary and significant events in our life. These significant events could be joyous or sorrowful. They might include marriage, births of children, death of a loved one, or significant health issues.

Although I never had a term to describe them before reading Marcus Borg, I have experienced thin places throughout my life. Singer/songwriter Harry Chapin brought me to a thin place listening to his story songs at a concert when I was in high school. When Barbara (my girlfriend at the time) and I heard his song "Mr. Tanner," we cried to the sadness and melancholic story of a struggling singer from Dayton, Ohio. Harry had a way of bringing my family and me to unexpected thin places. Songs from our childhood or young adult years often elicit a thin place and a moment in time recollected of joy or sadness. Our first child, Conor, was born May 25, 1984, when we were twenty-six years old. It was a thin place where the boundaries of creation were blurred. As the days passed, I wondered if we alone created this little newborn, or was some help from our creator involved?

Spending time with nature brings us to thin places. During the three trips with my kids, we all experienced thin places in our beautiful surroundings. Nature allowed us to reflect and meditate on the wonder of time and the thousands of years during which natural landscapes were formed.

Now that you understand what thin places are, what majestic or natural landscape places have you visited that evoke a thin place for you? What songs or sounds allow you to "visit" a thin place?

Through the thin places of our lives, we have the opportunity to pay attention, reflect, and be in the moment. Thin places provide a vehicle to breathe deeply while off the treadmill of life. We experience a unique ability in these thin places to be one with ourselves and who or what we believe to be the divine or creator. What an opportunity to embrace and notice thin places as often as possible.

We have worked through five techniques to assist us in reflecting daily. Gratefulness comes naturally for me, and I find ways to be grateful every day. Practicing gratefulness is my foundation for reflection on a daily basis. Breathing, our second technique, is something I struggle with. Through writing this book, I consistently visited my peaceful, quiet place and breathed deeper and more mindfully. I still struggle with making it a regular occurrence. We discussed meditation through the lens of the definition and a few stories about Barbara and me. I do not meditate, although I believe it is an important way to reflect daily. Next, we discussed rituals. They provide structure and keep us grounded. Our last technique for reflecting daily is thin places and God moments, where our hearts are opened and a veil is lifted between earth and the divine. Today, I feel humbled and grateful because I frequently am offered an opportunity to experience thin places. For me, these revelatory moments resonate profoundly and continue to have an impactful role in my life.

When we pay attention, we can look beyond the surface like a microscope and reflect on our day. Daily reflection is crucial to regenerate, learn, and reduce stress. It is a tool that enables us to introspectively target our hearts, minds, and souls.

Reflecting Daily can be cultivated any time during the day. For some, it's during your waking hours, and others at night before you sleep. Find the best time for you and practice one or all techniques discussed.

Our last tool is *Forgiveness*. Start with realizing we may have good intentions yet did not practice any reflective thought for the day. Forgive yourself without judgment and move on to tomorrow and the next chapter.

CHAPTER SEVEN

Forgive

So far, we have accumulated four tools in our kit. The first tool, *Pay Attention*, is the foundation of all our tools. This equates with the blueprint Dad utilized to build homes and commercial spaces. Next, we included *Utilize Goals* (the level), *Start Simply* (the hammer), and *Reflect Daily* (the microscope of our life). The last tool in our kit, *Forgive*, is the most difficult tool to utilize, let alone master. It is comparable to a retractable tape measure. Dad used a retractable tape measure many times a day in his work.

A tape measure is made of flexible, lightweight aluminum; the tool is malleability at its finest: it retracts, measures, extends. Flexibility is a critical aspect of forgiveness. If we have rigid beliefs, it is challenging to forgive. We need to be flexible and open to possibilities and change. Forgiveness is fundamental to this process and can help lead us there.

Imagine this: An unused tape measure is coiled up inside the case. Over time, and with kind patience, the device's flexibility and stretch can be effectively used. Similar to a tape measure, if we do not actively practice forgiveness, we can be constrained, wound up like a fully retracted coil. There is often initial resistance as we pull the end of the tape to measure something. Often we need to be "pulled" into forgiveness. When you push the retractable button on the case, the tape rapidly winds back up. Forgiveness can easily be "lost" as the tape rewinds back to where we started before we forgave ourselves or someone else. Think of the effort and commitment one must devoutly pursue in order for any forgiveness to become fully embraced. The delicacy of the tape measure provides an ideal example of this tenuous ebb and flow.

According to the dictionary, forgiveness is:

1. To grant pardon for or remission of (an offense, debt, etc.); absolve

2. To give up all claim on account of; remit (a debt, obligation, etc.)

3. To grant pardon to (a person).

4. To cease to feel resentment against: *to forgive one's enemies.*

5. To cancel an indebtedness or liability of: to forgive the interest owed on a loan.

All the definitions are applicable and appropriate for forgiveness. I will be sharing some personal stories and others' stories about forgiveness. First, let's discuss what forgiveness is not.

- **Forgiveness is not denial.** It is not forgiveness when we ignore the pain caused by trauma, abuse, or a life-changing event. This kind of numbness can in fact be the antithesis of true forgiveness. Perhaps too often bitterness and anger become our normal behaviors in life. We may not even know the trauma or pain occurred and how significant it resonates in our daily life.

- **Forgiveness is not weakness.** On the contrary, forgiveness is the ultimate in emotional strength, mental toughness, and well-being. It requires a broad perspective as well as understanding the other side of a story.

For me, forgiveness is ceasing to feel resentment; letting go of the anger, despair, and sadness I've experienced.

Dr. Bessel van der Kolk's book *The Body Keeps the Score*, discusses what trauma does to the body, mind, and spirit. Trauma can be perpetrated by a human being, an event such as an auto accident, or experiencing the ravages and horrors of war. Discussing several examples of trauma, he authenticates various therapies are necessary to eventually heal the trauma. It is possible for trauma to incapacitate us for months, years, and even a lifetime, yet we hope it does not define us. Discovering and finding help is sometimes a lifelong journey.

The shattering of our mental and emotional health occurs when we are not able to acknowledge and/or address trauma and pain. Over time, healing occurs through working with the correct therapies. It is the opposite of denial. It is uncovering the pain, sitting with the pain, acknowledging it, and realizing we will not die from it. It is possible to eventually forgive ourselves and the perpetrators or events that caused sorrow, sadness, and trauma. The real-life stories from Bessel's book are inspiring, although at times deeply sad, depressing, and sometimes unfathomable. Ultimately, we must learn to love ourselves and find emotional and mental health before we can forgive others or ourselves.

Forgiveness requires high self-awareness; the opposite, the self-involvement and narrow-mindedness of a narcissist. The ability to reflect and ask for help is necessary. Forgiveness may be a short process or one that takes a lifetime. Sometimes it is conscious and/or unconscious.

Forgiving yourself is about moving past the pain, past the hurt, past the self-talk that we are no good. It allows us to start the hour or the day or the month fresh and new. Start where you are and *Start Simply*. Only starting where you are allows you to move forward.

How do we *Forgive*? Forgiveness has historically been, and often continues to be, an ongoing struggle for humankind. Humans have been doing despicable and unspeakable things to other human beings since we evolved. Being human implies we are not perfect. We make mistakes, display cruelty to strangers and people we love, hold grudges, and are often self-centered. We offend friends and families knowingly and unknowingly. Human beings are a wondrous and perplexing paradox of behaviors.

Archbishop Desmond Tutu, in his book *The Book of Forgiving*, suggests a four-step process for forgiveness. His steps are:

1. Tell the story
2. Name the hurt
3. Grant forgiveness
4. Renew or release the relationship

Let us take a closer look at these four steps. The first step, *telling our story*, allows us to acknowledge the need for us to begin the process of forgiveness. Sharing our story can be with a friend, relative, spouse, or a therapist. For example, the first step in alcoholics anonymous is the admission of being an alcoholic. We tell our story. I will discuss my own stories later in this chapter.

In *The Body Keeps the Score*, van der Kolk discusses his work with Vietnam veterans. At the time of the Vietnam War, we did not have the term post-traumatic stress disorder (PTSD). It was not part of our vernacular. In 1980, PTSD was defined by the American Psychiatric Association. Group therapy was the method for the veterans to share their trauma stories with one another and Dr. van der Kolk.

Almost all the veterans he worked with suffered from PTSD. Healing was facilitated through sharing intense stories filled with raw emotion over the course of months and years. Various therapies discussed by Dr. van der Kolk were necessary for true healing. Many veterans from recent wars still suffer from post-traumatic stress disorder.

Knowing the stories of our families is important for children and family's emotional health. Robin Fivush, PhD, and Marshall Duke, PhD, psychologists from Emory University, began exploring resilience in children two decades ago. They created a twenty-question "Do You Know (DYN) Scale." The more children were aware of the stories of their family's history, including the good, bad, sad, and the traumatic, the more resilient the children turned out to be. Knowing their family stories turned out to be the best single predictor of children's emotional health and happiness.

Desmond Tutu further helps elucidate the terms of forgiveness. Tutu suggests our stories need to include feelings when we "name the hurt." This is step number two. Ignoring our emotions and feelings of pain can only become more debilitating and eventually control our life. Sharing emotions and feelings of the harm, trauma, and behaviors of others or ourselves is therapeutic and necessary to continue to heal and eventually forgive. This is "sitting with the pain." When we are in touch with our feelings, perhaps we will be sad, depressed, or even liberated.

In her book *Dignity*, Donna Hicks demonstrates words do cause harm. Neuroscientists have shown a psychological wound and a physical wound stimulate the same part of the brain. We heard as children, "sticks and stones may break my bones but words will never hurt me." This glib cliché is, in fact not true. As Hicks discovered, words are harmful and often devastating and/or lethal, according to today's research.

As we tell our stories and describe our hurt feelings, it is possible to grant forgiveness. *Granting forgiveness* is step three in Desmond Tutu's book. The process does not have to be linear. When bitterness, sadness, and uncontrollable behaviors overcome us, we can "sit" with these feelings and begin to let go and forgive. It is a conscious choice, but extremely challenging.

Prayer is often helpful, as are the tools and techniques outlined in the previous chapter, *Reflecting Daily* (gratefulness, breathing, meditation, daily rituals, thin places). When we accept the reality of the situation that caused harm, we let go and realize the past cannot be changed. Choosing to move forward, we live the life beyond the hurt, pain, and trauma.

We all experience pain and suffering in our life. This is part of living and aging. The choice is how we respond to the pain and suffering we have experienced.

Archbishop Tutu was appointed chair of South Africa's Truth and Reconciliation commission in 1994. He pioneered a new way of moving forward for South Africa.

After experiencing severe oppression, apartheid, and civil conflict, the nation chose a stupendous and wondrous path. Instead of retribution, vengeance, and violence, the path was to grant forgiveness (third step of Tutu's book) and move forward to heal South Africa's many ailments, maladies, wickedness, and collective hurt.

Archbishop Tutu's fourth step suggests we *release or renew the relationship* that has caused the suffering. This may include relationships with ourselves, others, or devastating events. We all have a shared humanity. This final step in forgiveness provides closure.

So, the question arises: Why do we need to forgive? Forgiveness encompasses forgiving ourselves and forgiving others. When we forgive others and ourselves, we release resentment, anger, vindictiveness, and other harmful, negative emotions stored in our mind and body. Forgiving is not easy and requires patience. Throughout our lives, forgiving is difficult work. Jean-Jacques Rousseau stated, "Patience is bitter, but its fruit is sweet."

Forgiveness moves us from denial to liberation. We are no longer tethered to the people or events that caused us harm. The perpetrators no longer control our lives. Captaining our own ships, we release ourselves from the bondage of hatred, sadness, and vengeance for the perpetrators and/or events.

What do we accomplish when we choose to forgive?

It is the ultimate in letting go. It is surrendering and accepting that as human beings, we are fallible, will err, make bad decisions, and not always serve ourselves in the best way possible. In short, forgiveness necessitates accepting we are human beings and imperfect.

The Serenity Prayer, by American theologian Reinhold Niebuhr, states this concept well:

> God, grant me the serenity to accept the things I cannot change,
>
> Courage to change the things I can,
>
> And wisdom to know the difference.

Some things we can change, and many we cannot. It is a fine line between what we can and cannot change as human beings. Discerning what is within our power to change is a challenging aspect of with forgiveness in life.

Harold Kushner's book, *When Bad Things Happen to Good People*, was an enlightening book for me and millions of others. At the age of three, his son was diagnosed with a premature aging disease. The doctors told Rabbi Harold Kushner his son would not live beyond his early teenage years. He wrote the book as a catharsis for himself and others who have been hurt and traumatized by life. The power of prayer assisted him as he grappled with this terrible news.

Prayer from friends, family, and the community helped Rabbi Kushner through this tragedy as he realized he was not alone in his grief. Forgiving God was difficult. As a rabbi, his faith was challenged because he could not understand why this had happened. Eventually, he realized God is not responsible for all things that occur to humans. Bad things happen to both good and bad people, and often there is no logic. How you cope and move through tragedy with shared love and prayer is a key message in his book.

Unbroken, the book by Laura Hillenbrand, is the life story of Louis Zamperini. Zamperini grew up as a troublemaker in Torrance, California, and turned his life around through running. As a teenager, he made the United States Olympic team and participated in the 1936 Olympic games in Berlin. The book and movie highlight his World War II experience as a prisoner of war (POW). After their fighter plane was shot down, Zamperini and his pilot friend Phil Phillips survived forty-six days in shark-infested waters in the Pacific Ocean. They were found by the Japanese and imprisoned for more than two years in several Japanese POW camps. The worst camp experience for Louis was with a sadistic guard named "Bird." The horrific stories of torture included public humiliation and interrogation, daily beatings, and lying face-down in excrement.

Although he returned home a war hero, it was a very difficult and tenuous transition. His pain was a terrible burden. Shackled to his POW story, his heart was torn as he was reacquainted with freedom.

Later, Zamperini married Cynthia Applewhite. They had two children, Luke and Cynthia. Unfortunately, he began to drink heavily, was haunted by regular nightmares, and suffered from untreated post-traumatic stress disorder. His marriage collapsed and seemed to be ending. As a desperate last resort, Cynthia asked him to attend a Billy Graham Crusade. Graham was a religious figure and Christian evangelist for over forty years. Attending numerous times, Louis turned his life over to Jesus Christ.

Thereafter, Zamperini quit drinking and reconciled with his wife. Years later he began the process of forgiving his captors. It took many years and many challenges for Louis Zamperini to forgive the people who had regularly tortured him. He returned to Japan decades later to forgive his captors in person. The notorious guard "Bird" refused to meet with him. He was able to see other guards and verbally offered them his forgiveness. It is an example of forgiveness almost unfathomable to those privy to his experience. If I were Louis, I do not know if I could have forgiven what the guards in the camp had done to me and the other American serviceman.

Mr. Zamperini became a motivational speaker, carried the Olympic torch for several games, and started a non-for-profit "Victory Boys Camp" dedicated to helping at-risk youth. This became his life's work until he died a few years ago at age ninety-seven.

~

Barbara and I have been involved in an organization through our church called "Hands of Peace." Their mission statement reads: "Hands of Peace is an interfaith organization that empowers young people to raise their voices as leaders of change. Through the power of dialogue, Palestinians, Israelis, and Americans partner to pursue peace, equality, freedom and justice. Hands of Peace believe the future depends on the leadership of the next generation." Founded by three Chicago-area women (one Christian, one Jewish, and one Muslim), it is an interfaith organization dedicated to nurturing peace, person by person.

Over the last many years, Barbara and I hosted three Palestinian boys (Mohammed, Ahmed, and Basheer) when they were in high school. Two of them lived in the West Bank and one lived in San Diego. Discussions between teenagers of Muslim, Jewish, and Christian faiths revolved around the ongoing conflict between Israeli Jews and Palestinian Muslims and Christians. They talked about their own stories of hurt, understanding the "other side," learning other narratives of their common histories, and being a part of the peace process. (Professional facilitators assist students in the program through these intense discussions every day.)

Mohammed, our first boy we hosted, was a sixteen-year-old Palestinian Muslim and had never met a Jew. He was motivated to understand the other side.

Mohammed lives in Nablus, a city in the West Bank. There was an uprising, or *intifada*, when he was seven years old. Israeli soldiers occupied his hometown for months. It was guerilla warfare between the Israeli Defense Forces (IDF) and Palestinians. Now he better understands the conflict and is working hard to make a difference. Mohammed has not forgiven the Israeli government. He understands his own story and the physical and emotional hurts, but is not ready to forgive the Israeli government. He genuinely wants to be part of the solution for peace and end the Israeli occupation. Mohammed wants to make a difference through his involvement with Hands of Peace. He and Ahmed continue to be active participants in the program.

It was difficult for us to witness our boys and other Palestinians viewed as second-class citizens by many Israelis. Barbara and I understand both sides have perpetrated horrendous acts of murder and terror on each other. Mohammed and Ahmed are the first to acknowledge the hurt on both sides of this conflict. Wanting only a free Palestine, they truly are wiser than their age and carry the torch of understanding through peace to move forward as a culture.

In 2016, Barbara and I visited Israel and the West Bank. It was a life-changing, momentous, and emotional trip. We now more clearly understand the struggles between Israelis and Palestinians. Although we spent two weeks in Israel and the West Bank, we felt we needed more time. As Christians, we were excited to see the sights of Jesus Christ—where he walked, preached, and died. Visiting our boys in their homes in the West Bank was wonderful and emotional. Understanding their struggles of daily life as Muslims and Palestinians in the West Bank, surrounded by checkpoints and Israeli settlements, was eye-opening. Leaving the West Bank, Barbara, Mustafa (our driver) and I were stopped at a checkpoint and asked to exit our car. The IDF checked the entire vehicle and looked at our passports several times. We stood and waited while soldiers with machine guns walked around the checkpoint area and our vehicle. We were scared and worried. Would we be delayed or arrested? After forty-five long minutes, we were allowed to pass through the checkpoint and continued our trip. This was a small glimmer of what many Palestinians live with every day. We understood their lives much better and never anticipated the thin places and God moments experienced in their hometowns.

Barbara and I are profoundly proud of all the participants in the HOP program. The stories of sadness, injustice, death, and hope on both sides are all too frequent. The skills the participants are learning and practicing center on peace and critical thinking, today and in the future.

A remarkable story from Desmond Tutu's book about Bassam Aramin, a Palestinian, from Hebron, a city in the West Bank, is uplifting. He was twelve years old when he watched an Israeli soldier kill another twelve-year-old boy. Later he joined a group of freedom fighters in Hebron. Some called him a freedom fighter and others a terrorist. At seventeen, he was caught planning an attack on Israeli Army troops and was sentenced to seven years in prison. In captivity, often stripped naked and regularly beaten by the prison guards, his hatred increased.

While in prison, Bassam engaged in a continual dialogue with his Israeli guard. Through time and conversation, they both realized how much they had in common. Bassam says it was the first time he had felt empathy in his life. His epiphany was the realization violence would never bring peace. This experience changed his life.

In 2005, Bassam Aramin cofounded a group called Combatants for Peace. Another tragedy occurred in 2007. An Israeli soldier shot his ten-year-old daughter, Abir, outside her school. Here is his response to this tragedy: "Abir's murder could have led me down the easy path of hatred and vengeance, but for me there was no return from dialogue and nonviolence. After all, it was one Israeli soldier who shot my daughter, but one hundred former Israeli soldiers who built a garden in her name at the school where she was murdered." Is there a better example of forgiveness in today's world?

"Amazing Grace," the well-known spiritual song, has a fascinating and unexpected story behind the author. Written by an Englishman, John Newton, it was published in 1779. Newton wrote the song from personal experience. Newton first served in the Royal Navy and eventually became involved in the slave trade. In 1748, his vessel was severely battered off the coast of Ireland. He called out to God for mercy. He had a spiritual conversion to Christianity that day, although he continued his slave trade career until 1755. He began studying Christian theology and was ordained in the Anglican Church in 1764. Twenty years later, he finally renounced the slave trade. He was instrumental in abolishing the slave trade in the early nineteenth century.

The song's message of forgiveness and redemption regardless of our past behaviors and transgressions is inspirational, emotional, and based on fact.

In my own life, the message of forgiveness has ebbed and flowed from my youth until today.

I was fortunate to play three years of college baseball and two-and-a-half seasons of college football. I was red-shirted my sophomore year of football, which gave me an additional year to play baseball. When I was recruited for football, the coaches promised I could play baseball in the winter and spring after my freshman season of football. Most division one sports programs require year-round training, so I was delighted to play two sports.

The football coaches reneged on the promise I could play baseball my sophomore year. Playing winter baseball my sophomore year, I needed to return to spring football in lieu of playing baseball in the spring. The baseball team went to the college World Series that year. The head coach was Dick Seibert, and his teams had been to several college World Series and were national champs in 1956, 1960, and 1964. Dave Winfield and Paul Moliter, future hall-of-fame baseball players, played for Dick. Dick Siebert played for the legendary Connie Mack in professional baseball and learned deep and insightful baseball statistics well before Billy Beane of the Oakland A's professional baseball team made it famous.

Six weeks into my junior year, the football coaches wanted me back on the scout team for an upcoming game. I felt angry, betrayed, and distraught. My response: I told the coaches 'no;' I had had enough. I *Started Simply* (tool number 3) by making an appointment with Mr. Paul Giel, our athletic director. I let him know I was quitting football and going to play baseball full-time. Bruised, battered, and exhausted from my football experience, I explained to him the team was going to lose a good teammate with a great attitude. I also emphatically told him the scholarship was mine through the school term.

When I left football and started playing baseball, it was like a gorilla had been lifted off my back. I had been on the football scout team for two full years. As a running back, my job during grueling practices was to play the other team's running back against our starting defense. My freshman year, I had even pretended to be Archie Griffith, who was a two-time Heisman Trophy winner for Ohio State. While today, I can reflect and feel gratefulness, it was a difficult process to quit.

I had to forgive myself for quitting football. Quitting had never been in my vocabulary. My parents had taught me to continue to work hard and good things would eventually happen. Earning an athletic scholarship had reinforced my hard work. I'd loved running the football in junior high and high school. Although it was fun my freshman year playing on the scout team, by my junior year, I dreaded attending practice.

Joining the baseball team in the middle of fall practice was a critical turning point in my life. Feeling like a kid again, jumping into practice, playing a game I had loved since a young child, I was imbued with gratefulness and joy.

It was exciting playing for such a legendary and accomplished coach as Dick Siebert. Sadly, Coach Siebert died at the end of my junior year. His assistant, George Thomas, became the head coach. This was another extraordinary turning point in my life. I had no idea how Coach Thomas would change my life. George is still my "coach" and I am lucky to call him a friend. For me, George was a great coach and mentor. Many of my behaviors and philosophies of dealing with adversity, I owe to him. He continues to be a major influence in my life. George has an astonishing ability to be positive in the face of adversity. One of my favorite sayings of his is, "If this is the worst thing to happen today, we will be OK." George is now battling leukemia and doing well. He continues to amaze me with his positive attitude and hilarious sense of humor.

Playing three years of baseball, captain and MVP my last year, was beyond what I had imagined when I left football. Quitting football allowed me to have success in baseball. My destiny was forever changed. Forgiving myself for quitting football changed my life and brought this very special person, George Thomas into my life.

As previously discussed in the Wheel of Life, relationships are critical in my life. My family is the most important part of my life. When we grant forgiveness in our relationships, we recognize our shared humanity. When we hold on to the grudges, anger, and bitterness, it negatively impacts our overall health and our cherished relationships.

Conor, our oldest child and only son, suffered from a terrible trauma when he was thirteen years old. For more than three years, we did not know about this. As I mentioned, we have three daughters, all younger than Conor. Conor began to experience anger issues about a year after the trauma. As he entered high school, we thought his behavior was adolescence and the adjustment to high school. He eventually started to see a clinical psychologist. Although the therapist helped, Conor's behavior worsened his sophomore and junior year of high school. In January of his junior year (he was sixteen-and-a-half) we were asked by his therapist to come to a session with Conor.

I do not remember the specific day in January, but I remember leaving her office with Barbara shocked, angry, and dismayed. Conor shared he had "sex" with the family babysitter. During that session, Conor had told us, "I am done dealing with this; now you can deal with it." We did not anticipate how this statement would resonate for Conor and our whole family until this day. The babysitter (Mary—not her real name) had been nineteen when she perpetrated sexual abuse for over six months on our recently-turned thirteen-year-old son. We were horrified, shocked, angry, filled with rage, and devastated. For more than three years, Conor had kept this secret from all of us. He had only told his therapist several months prior to our meeting with her.

We focused on assisting Conor and our entire family through this horrific unforeseen traumatic experience: it was a trauma for all of us. Barbara and I felt like terrible parents. This happened on our watch and in our own home. Conor thought this was love, not sexual abuse.

We began to understand why Conor's behavior had become more self-destructive when he entered high school; he had lost his innocence, as it was violently stolen from him when he turned thirteen years old. His anger eventually became uncontrollable and unpredictable. He articulated that regular pot-smoking at least masked the pain for several hours.

In retrospect, it was the most challenging time for our marriage, family, and for Conor. Three weeks after he told us about the sexual abuse, we overheard him talking to his ex-girlfriend on the phone. She had been his girlfriend from the middle of eighth grade through freshman year. They began dating shortly after the six months of sexual abuse ended. The overheard phone conversation was extremely unsettling to Barbara and me. Conor was talking about hurting himself. We called the therapist and she told us to go immediately to the hospital. I still remember her words: "You need to go; you will be able to dry these tears."

This began the tumultuous, arduous long journey of healing and forgiveness for Conor, Barbara, our daughters, and me. It was not easy to share this trauma with our families and friends but in doing so we asked for their prayers for Conor and our family. Under severe adversity, discovering genuine love and support from family, friends, our church and our creator was miraculous and healing. Bearing the pain alone is frightening and unnecessary. All of us are vulnerable. Acknowledging this leads to healing. When we involve loved ones, we share the burdens, heal, and grow together as one human family.

Barbara and I knew Conor needed more intense

therapy to begin recovering from this trauma. We worked with several professionals to find the best fit for Conor. It was an emotional roller coaster. At the end of his junior year of high school, we found a program for him. We had him escorted to an emotional-growth wilderness program in Utah called "Second Nature." I was the only one home with Conor at 4:30 in the morning when two physically large and intimidating escorts took him to the airport and the program in Utah. After they left, I drove to the lakefront and watched the sun rise over Lake Michigan. I cried for a long time that morning. Although it took about one week, Conor eventually immersed himself in this program for the summer.

The sixty days Conor was in Utah was fraught with uneasiness, anxiety, extreme sadness, depression, and hope for our entire family. While Conor was in Utah, our family was traumatized and fractured. Because letter-writing was the only means of communicating with Conor, we exchanged letters frequently. Once a week, we talked with the therapist in the program about Conor's progress. According to the therapist, Conor fully immersed himself in the program and reached a level few teenagers ever reach in their program. It was a long journey heading toward the unknown with Conor's mental and emotional health. He processed his issues and worked extremely hard. Realizing he was only seventeen, we felt he needed more therapy.

We wanted him to attend a different high school to

receive more specific attention for emotional and mental support. For a myriad of reasons, this secondary program in late August did not work out as planned. These unforeseen circumstances changed things and ultimately he returned home at the end of the summer. Conor attended his senior year at his high school and graduated with his class. It ended up being the perfect decision for both Conor and our family. We loved one another and needed to be together.

Words cannot express how proud I am of my son Conor. He has worked on his emotional, physical, and mental well-being since the trauma occurred. He became a Fulbright Scholar several years ago, is finishing his PhD in art history at Stanford, and has done many other amazing and noteworthy things in his young life. Conor is sensitive, brilliant, a wonderful son, and a tremendous human being.

It has taken a long time for me to forgive myself for not seeing this abuse occurring during the six-month time frame. Our family has been forever impacted by the sexual abuse perpetrated on Conor. We attended family therapy with Conor before he left for Utah, while he was in Utah, and when he returned. We learned how secrets are so damaging to the core being of a young thirteen-year-old boy and his family. What happened to Conor at thirteen, he was not able to process as abuse. When our son was in Utah, I can remember the family therapist asking Taylor, who was entering fifth grade at the time, "How are you doing, Taylor?" Taylor welled up with tears in her eyes and said, "I just want to know what is going on." Barbara and I thought we communicated age-appropriately to Taylor what had happened to Conor. Clearly, we had not communicated well enough. Navigating this stressful, unchartered territory was immensely difficult.

The family therapy gave all of us a voice to talk about the trauma and work through our healing. Conor was doing his own emotional and physical work: hiking, backpacking, cooking his own meals, daily group therapy with other adolescents, and individual therapy once a week with a trained clinician. The Second Nature program saved our son. We chose to have him airlifted out of the toxic environment of Glenview for intensive daily therapy. If he had stayed in Glenview, we will never know if he would have been able to make the progress he made in Utah. I believe we made the right decision and saved our son's life.

Conor embraced the program as we hoped and prayed he was capable of doing. He made amazing progress, as I mentioned earlier. He began to heal. Yet several questions haunted Barbara and me. When Conor returned home, how would his emotional health be? Was it possible to have the son back we knew and loved? We had countless sleepless nights worrying and wondering how Conor was doing. What should the next steps be to ensure his overall health?

As parents, our job is to protect and love our children not only when they are young, but as they grow and mature. I had failed as a father to protect my son when he was a young thirteen-year-old adolescent. When I look at photos of Conor at thirteen, when this abuse started, I am sickened, saddened, and cry. Friends and family asked us if we would prosecute the perpetrator. We never pursued filing charges.

At the time, we believed the most important thing was to help Conor and our family heal. I have thought about Mary through the years. I have been able to tell the story and name the hurt, and I believe I've released the relationship. I think she was abused, but I am not certain. Because she carries the burden of being a sexual abuser, I hope she is in therapy. The process of writing about these scarring memories and writing this traumatic history has been therapeutic for me. Confronting the past and the process of healing has helped me forgive her. But I have not yet forgiven her completely. This has resonated for nineteen years. Sometimes I believe I have forgiven her of this insidious criminal act, and other times I am angry and sad for Conor and our family. I pray forgiveness will heal all of us in time.

We have participated in family therapy sessions, as the kids have become adults. It has been therapeutic, emotional, and very difficult. About five years ago, I asked Conor to forgive me. We had an emotional discussion on the porch at home. Conor told me, "It was OK, Dad. I forgive you and I love you." This began a healing process to forgive myself. We are all human. I love my son as only a father can. We both continue therapy in various ways and will continue to work

127

through the pain, suffering, and forgiveness.

Forgiving Conor was also a part of my journey. Why did he keep this a secret? Why did he not tell Barbara and me? He was thirteen and participated in the abuse that he told himself was love and a healthy relationship. As I looked at his thirteen-year-old photos, I realized how young he was and could not process this as abuse. It allowed me to gradually forgive him for keeping this a secret. He did not know what to do. It took courage, grace, and the right timing for Conor to come forward with the truth.

Conor's own story of the abuse has changed over time. He believed this was love for many years. During a family therapy session a few years ago, he acknowledged maybe it was abuse and love. Today, I believe he realizes this was sexual abuse perpetrated on a child by an adult.

~

Forgiveness may be the most difficult and challenging emotion and action we embrace as humans. M. Scott Peck, author of *The Road Less Traveled*, says in the first line of the book, "life is difficult." Forgiveness is extremely hard work. A Gaelic proverb states, "Nothing is easy for the unwilling." The journey of forgiveness requires our willing participation, and it is demanding and burdensome.

Stories of forgiveness are inspiring and sometimes even astounding. When I think of Bassam Aramin, it is prodigious and mind-boggling he could forgive his captors and a murderer of his young daughter. If he can forgive guards for beatings and an Israeli soldier for murdering his ten-year-old daughter, can I forgive Mary? I am on the road to forgiving her for the reverberating sorrow and sadness she is responsible for. Writing this chapter has been cathartic.

Who do you need to forgive in your life? Will it make you a better human being if you forgive someone you never thought you would or could forgive?

FORGIVENESS

1. Write the names of people you want to forgive.

_____

_____

_____

_____

_____

_____

_____

_____

_____

_____

2. Write the names of people who you feel need forgiveness for something you have done.

_____

_____

_____

_____

_____

_____

_____

_____

_____

3. Reflect on Desmond Tutu's four steps: A) Tell the story, B) Name the hurt, C) Grant forgiveness, D) Renew or release the relationship, event or circumstances.

4. Select one of the names you want to forgive.

   _____

5. Share the story with a close friend, therapist, or whomever you are comfortable with.

6. Reflect about this person and the circumstances of what they did to you. It will help you fully understand why you need to forgive them.

7. Name the hurt and write your emotions and feelings.

   _____

   _____

   _____

   _____

   _____

   _____

   _____

   _____

   _____

   _____

   _____

   _____

   _____

8. Can you grant forgiveness yet? If so, determine how you will proceed. Will you do this alone, or will you share this with the perpetrator?

9. Can you renew or release the relationship? If so, choose to renew or release the relationship.

10. Remind yourself forgiveness is a lifelong process and at times is difficult. The four steps are not linear.

Forgiveness and its lessons come from our own lives, literature, movies, and sacred religious writings. A central tenet of many religions, forgiveness requires love, kindness, and trust. It is a choice that leads to our emotional, physical, and spiritual health. When we do not forgive, we can become sad, depressed, and emotionally out of balance. This can poison our relationships with our children, parents, siblings, spouses, friends, and relatives.

If we can learn how to forgive in our personal relationships, perhaps we can recognize our shared humanity. Holding grudges and displaying anger negatively impacts our health.

A portion of the Our Father or the Lord's Prayer in the Christian faith speaks of forgiveness. "Forgive us our trespasses (debts) as we forgive those who trespass against us (as we have forgiven our debtors)." If God our creator forgives us, why can't we forgive others and ourselves?

We all need to forgive and be forgiven throughout our lifetimes. Healthy and stable human beings practice forgiveness regularly. Realizing no one is perfect and we fail repeatedly as human beings is emotionally healthy. We have and will make mistakes and behave badly in our lives. Some are minor and some may seem to be unforgivable. All are about the acceptance of being human.

M. Scott Peck, in *The Road Less Traveled*, says, "The truth is that our finest moments are most likely to occur when we are feeling deeply uncomfortable, unhappy, or unfulfilled. For it is only in such moments, propelled by our discomfort, that we are most likely to step out of our ruts and start searching for different ways or truer answers."

For me, this quote speaks clearly about the power of forgiveness. When we forgive, we find the truth. We are all broken as human beings, and forgiveness makes us whole human beings again and again.

Exploring forgiveness is a challenge and a lifelong process. Tell your story to someone and sit with the hurt and pain. As you grant forgiveness, may you release or renew the relationship involved.

Getting off the treadmill, uncovering your life's purpose and mission can be daunting and a challenging experience. Use each tool in your kit individually or collectively to complete the job of living an intentional and fulfilling life of purpose.

Our last two chapters incorporate all five tools and two more fundamental ideas: I call these *Taking the High Road* and *Being Good Tired* at the end of each day.

CHAPTER EIGHT

Take the High Road

Our tool kit is now complete. Before we delve into chapter eight, *Take the High Road*, it is an opportune time to review each of the five tools in our belt.

As you recall, our first tool is *Pay Attention*. Paying attention, like my father's blueprint, is the anchor. It includes curiosity and focused observation of our surroundings. It is also about paying attention to our actions and increasing self-awareness. The second tool, *Utilizing Goals*, is similar to my Dad's level and critical to stability: leading an intentional, purposeful and fulfilling life. *Starting Simply* is number three. Like the hammer, it is a necessary and basic tool. It is easy to hammer away and not pay attention. Starting simply implies the cliché, "start where you are;" there is no need to get ahead of yourself. You cannot begin training for a marathon without first walking or running small distances.

Tool number four, *Reflecting Daily*, allows us the ability to self-assess each and every day of our life. The microscope, similar to daily reflections, provides a laser focus beyond what the naked eye views. Although my father did not use a microscope, he did have a magnifying glass. This allowed him to see things clearly. All of us have methodologies to reflect. Whether it is gratefulness, breathing, meditation, rituals, or finding and experiencing thin places and God moments, a daily reflection rejuvenates us. Reflecting consistently invigorates all our devices (tools). Lastly, the retractable tape measure is similar to our final tool, *Forgiveness*. Forgiveness liberates us as human beings. We all need to forgive someone and to be forgiven. Forgiveness lifts us out of the fog and mud we are stuck in.

Finishing work for the day, my father placed his tool belt in the trunk of his car. Arriving home from work, he locked the trunk with a real key to keep his tools safe. Keyless entry did not exist at the time. The following morning, Dad's key allowed him to unlock and utilize all his tools during the day. *Taking the High Road* is the *key* that unlocks our tools to be employed each and every day of our life. When we *Take the High Road*, all the tools are unleashed.

What is taking the high road? Articulating the phrase, "take the high road" has been part of my language and belief system since college. My children have grown accustomed to hearing me say "take the high road." Taking the high road is a philosophy of life and incorporates all the tools in our belt.

Surprisingly, the phrase 'high road' has definitions in

several dictionaries. According to the dictionary, "high road" is defined as:

1. *chiefly Brit.* A main road; highway

2. an easy or direct way

3. a course of action, position, etc. that is *uninfluenced* by partisanship, self-interest, vindictiveness, etc., usually in the phrase *take the high road.*

The third definition resonates for me. It speaks to my heart. Relying on this meaning, we are *not* influenced by intolerance, vengefulness, or self-interest when we take the high road. We approach life as perpetual learners: naïve and vulnerable to the constant curiosities the world may offer. Life is an open filter of possibilities. When we live the philosophy of taking the high road, we can develop an insatiable desire for understanding people, cultures, history, and knowledge of the world.

We are objective and intentional listeners without judgments. It sounds utopian and unimaginable in our daily behaviors in life. While this perpetual state of kind generosity and benevolent spirit may indeed never be fully attainable, it is the struggle that imbues the process of the high road with meaning. This is why taking the high road is an ongoing challenge and struggle.

I realize the world may be cynical of the term *Take the High Road*. Possibly, it is overused in today's vernacular and has less meaning to the general population than to me. That said, there is often profound meaning in the *everyday*. Perhaps, in fact, overused clichés resonate with culture for reasons never fully understandable or articulated. I hope this chapter can shed light on taking the high road and the misguided glibness often attributed to this righteous idea.

Like forgiveness, it is a lifelong process of successes and failures. We will be successful and fail many times choosing the path of the high road. But it is worthwhile attempting to master, because it is so rewarding and fulfilling.

Several key behaviors and characteristics are required to take the high road:

1. Humility

2. Seek first to understand

3. Selflessness

4. Boundless emotional, mental, and physical energy

5. Empathy

6. Well rounded perspective

7. Letting go of needing to be right

The first, humility, is foundational to taking the high road. When we have a modest opinion of ourselves, we are not arrogant or over-confidant. Humble individuals do not have any feeling of superiority to other people. We understand we are all part of the human race and equal in our creator's eyes. Humility is the opposite of boasting and bragging. It enhances and elevates all our tools.

Second, life is approached seeking first to understand, then to be understood. This is Steven Covey's fifth habit in his bestseller, *The 7 Habits of Highly Effective People*. We actively listen to the person speaking. Seeking first to understand necessitates paying attention. Intentionally taking another person's perspective through seeking first to understand, and not jumping to conclusions, is a cornerstone of taking the high road. We may ask clarifying questions with the intention to better comprehend. We need to be present and in the moment when listening, and do not provide feedback unless asked.

A third attribute of taking the high road is selflessness. Taking the high road places others first and ourselves second. My wife, Barbara, personified this when the kids were growing up. As mentioned previously, I have been dating or married to Barbara for forty-four years. I have observed with wonder and amazement my wife taking the high road with our family over the years. She always put the kids and me first with her loving behaviors and actions. Barbara infrequently puts herself first.

Today, we live in a world with the potential for self-absorption and self-centeredness. Social media fuels the ability to focus on "me." I believe it distracts us with less important behaviors, such as checking Facebook, Twitter accounts, and staring at a mobile device for long periods of time. We sometimes miss what is most important in life: interacting with human beings and making a difference in the world. Making a difference starts with our actions. A high-road philosophy followed by benevolent actions is powerful.

Barbara did not think less of herself for being selfless and laser-focused on raising our children in a loving environment. A quote from C.S. Lewis states it well; "Humility is not thinking less of yourself, it's thinking of yourself less."

Taking the high road requires boundless emotional, mental, and physical energy. This is our fourth characteristic. When we are focused with overall positive energy, it leads us to take the high road.

Not only was my wife a dedicated and loving mom to our four young children, she also finished her PhD before our youngest child, Taylor, was three. She had many reasons to regularly complain— sleep deprivation; sick, needy kids; a chaotic house with four young children; supporting me in a startup business; and struggling financially to make ends meet. She never complained, was amazingly dedicated to her family, and powerfully motivated to finish her doctorate in developmental psychology. Her endless energy and commitment to her family was evident throughout those years and continues today.

Currently, Barbara is a full time "Mimi"/grandma and takes care of Luke, our grandson. Seeing her interact with Luke Michael in a deliberate, loving, and passionate alpha state inspires me to pay attention and be present with Luke. Furthermore, our extended family calls Barbara a "baby whisperer." She has a gift of being completely present with babies and small children. Also, she has an enviable talent of soothing crying babies and sensing their unspoken needs. I still marvel at her energy level and stamina with infants and small children.

The fifth behavior necessary for the high road is empathy. When we take the high road, we feel compassion for others and their feelings. Empathy is analogous with listening and striving to understand people's true feelings without judgment. People who are empathetic use actions to fulfill specific needs for loved ones. In Brené Brown's book, *I Thought It Was Just Me (But It Isn't)*, she discusses Theresa Wiseman's four attributes of empathy.

They are:

1. To be able to see the world as others see it— This requires putting your own "stuff" aside to see the situation through your loved one's eyes.

2. To be nonjudgmental—Judgment of another person's situation discounts the experience and is an attempt to protect ourselves from the pain of the situation.

3. To understand another person's feelings—We have to be in touch with our own feelings in order to understand someone else's. Again, this requires putting your own "stuff" aside to focus on your loved one.

4. To communicate your understanding of that person's feelings—Rather than saying, "At least you..." or "It could be worse..." try, "I've been there, and that really hurts," or (to quote an example from Brown) "It sounds like you are in a hard place now. Tell me more about it."

If we are able to see the world as others see it, be nonjudgmental, truly understand a person's feelings, and be able to communicate those feelings, we accomplished taking the high road with another human being.

Maintaining a well-rounded perspective when life's challenges and hardships take their toll on us is important to be successful in following the path of the high road. This is our sixth characteristic and entails coping well with the joys and sorrows of life. We instill in our hearts and mind the philosophy of "this too shall pass" under challenging and distressing times. We do not routinely allow things to fester or bother us. We accept life's struggles as experiences from which to learn and grow. We can begin to understand very little in life is permanent.

The last characteristic necessary for taking the high

road is to let go of the need to be right. This narcissistic attitude prevents true growth as a human being. I am the fifth of eight children. Early in life I developed a strong sense of independence and felt I needed to take care of myself. I only asked for help when it was absolutely necessary. This led me to be very righteous and overly independent in thought and action. Because of this belief, in my youth, I had a hard time admitting I was wrong. I have made improvement over the years, yet still struggle with being righteous to family and friends. Taking the high road is inconsistent with this kind of righteousness.

Years ago, after dinner, I was cleaning the kitchen with the kids. Explaining to Barbara how I loaded the dishwasher, I stated "this is how you do it." Barbara looked at me incredulously and asked, sarcastically, "Oh, is this the Mike Lauesen way, the right way, the best way?" I laughed very hard. Taking the high road is the ability to hear criticism, genuinely reflect, and laugh at our myopic and narcissistic behaviors, similar to the "Mike Lauesen way" of loading the dishwasher.

Perhaps we are certain our facts are correct when engaging in a discussion with someone who has an opposite set of facts (has an opposing viewpoint). We make a conscious choice to take the high road and let it go. We ask more questions for a deeper understanding of where we may be wrong or misunderstood. These are sincere questions because we truly care and want to understand the individual's perspective. Learning is a sincere intention allowing personal growth.

Our tool kit is fully operational when we take the high road. We utilize our first tool, *Paying Attention*, on a daily basis to take the high road. When we are present and in the moment, it is difficult to be triggered out of our focused state. It is staying grounded and not shrinking under adversity or challenges. Our principles and ethics are the foundation we live by. The ideal state of mind for taking the high road is alpha, or our peaceful, quiet place. Where is your peaceful, quiet place? Close your eyes and go to your peaceful, quiet place and imagine yourself taking the high road.

The second tool in our kit, *Utilizing Goals*, is relevant to taking the high road. When we set our intention and goal to take the high road for the day, we will have a higher success rate. If we have a goal to be humbler and seek more to understand than be understood, are more empathetic, and let go of needing to be right, we will be successful in regularly taking the high road. What goal(s) can you set to take the high road?

Taking the high road begins with *Starting Simply*. We review each category of our life wheel and make a conscious choice of where we can start. Starting simply implies we can start with one category of our life wheel in taking the high road. Barbara started simply each evening in graduate school. Her dissertation writing started between 9:00 and 10:00 in the evening. The kids in bed, coffee made, she began to write. Often, she only finished a paragraph, and other nights she wrote several pages late into the evening. Either way, she started by making the coffee and sitting down at the table to begin. Is there a behavior or action you can *Start Simply* doing with the result of taking the high road?

Taking the high road requires *Daily Reflection*. As previously mentioned, gratefulness is part of my daily reflection. When we are grateful, we are receptive to taking the high road. What methods do you use to reflect, and in turn take the high road?

Forgiveness is the quintessential aspect of taking the high road. We seek to understand and center on humility and consider forgiveness as the ideal option. The philosophy of taking the high road is directly correlated to forgiveness. How close are you to taking the high road and starting the forgiveness process with someone?

Everyone has challenges throughout their life. These challenges are often significant and can be life-changing. Taking the high road under these circumstances is tenuous and difficult. We need to utilize all our tools.

More than twenty years ago, I began having regular back pain. Learning to live with it, I used massage and other therapies that were helpful to minimize it. One morning, I could not get out of bed due to the back pain. Several days later, I saw an orthopedic surgeon. After an X-ray, he assured me it was only muscle tightness with spasms and I would heal. In the following years, I lived my active life and, when needed, used ice, massage, and Advil as a remedy for pain.

Unfortunately, the pain crippled me a few more times in the following years. In April of 2013, the pain was debilitating. I made an appointment with my family doctor who recommended an integrative medical doctor who worked specifically with the spine area.

Limping gingerly into his office, I slowly and painfully hoisted myself onto the examining table. He performed a physical exam. I had an X-ray and later an MRI which revealed three vertebral compression fractures in my lumbar region. The doctor was perplexed. I was a fifty-five-year-old male, former athlete, and worked out regularly. He asked if I had had a car accident recently, or fallen off a ladder? These can cause compression fractures in the spine. The answer was "no."

He quickly ordered more tests: bone scan, bone density, numerous blood and urine tests. The doctors were trying to rule many things out. Some possible causes of such fractures are multiple myeloma, celiac disease, kidney, thyroid, or parathyroid issues.

I was diagnosed with severe osteoporosis. Osteoporosis is a disorder in which bones become porous and subject to fractures. It is thinning bone. Because the vertebrae are the thinnest bones in the body, osteoporosis is most often revealed in the spine, where many fractures occur. It is not life-threatening, but can make everyday life miserable. A vertebral fracture is painful and can take up to six months to completely heal. Now I understood why the last few years had entailed so much pain. I never knew I had fractured my back three times. Cycling and working out were impossible when a fracture was healing. I finally had an answer regarding the cause of my back pain.

The integrative doctor suggested I meet with a nephrologist—a kidney specialist. The nephrologist discovered I had idiopathic hypercalciuria. "Idiopathic" is a word that means "an unknown cause of a disease or condition." There are many diseases and conditions that can be idiopathic. Hypercalciuria is an excessive amount of calcium in the urine. The doctors call it leaking calcium. They guessed it had been present for decades. I had been losing bone over the past several decades and did not know it. It was a depressing time in my life.

Devastated, miserable, and angry, I began searching for answers and treatments. I was up all hours of the night for several weeks investigating information on the Internet about osteoporosis. Not only did I not take the high road, I often lashed out at Barbara. I faked it as best as I could around other people. But around Barbara and the kids, I was not a good person. I was mean, scared, confused, frustrated, and following the low road.

How could this happen to me? Strong and fit, I now needed help. Playing sports, my whole life had conditioned me to push through pain and adversity. Many questions raced through my mind. Was my active lifestyle going to change? Could I still cycle? Would I be able to play with my future grandchildren? Was I going to be bent over and crippled a few years from now? I found nothing to be grateful for and was depressed.

After several months, I had a thin-place experience. It was a God moment. Laboriously and in pain picking up after our dog Chapin, it hit me like a thunderbolt; I realized this was not a death sentence and was *lucky to be alive.*

When the doctor originally suggested it could be a multitude of causes, I was concerned. Multiple myeloma is a form of life threatening bone marrow cancer and was a possibility. With my God moment, it finally sunk in I did not have cancer and my condition was treatable. I was in a better frame of mind to accept my condition. To *only be* diagnosed with osteoporosis was a blessing, and I was thankful.

Grateful to be alive, I was back on the high road and thankful for the God moment waking me up. Instead of battling cancer with only several months to live, I now take medications to control the loss of calcium. I also changed my exercise routine. It has been a journey of ups and downs. Grief has several steps and I went through most of them: denial, anger, depression, and finally acceptance.

Accepting osteoporosis, I decided it would not define me. I could work my life around my "bad" bone density score. Alive and mending over time, I became abundantly grateful for my newfound attitude and physical health.

Because of osteoporosis, taking the high road taught me several key things. It was a blessing I did not see at the time. It was a thin place, and God was trying to get my attention to finally address my back pain. God's message resonated with me through picking up after Chapin.

Lessons are bountiful in life. I was not a ready student for several months after being diagnosed. Osteoporosis taught me to ask for help. When I need to lift certain things that are heavy or awkward and may cause a potential fracture, I ask for help. Osteoporosis gently reminded me of the blessing of mindfulness. I now mindfully and carefully walk, especially when it is raining or snowing. Paying attention more than ever to the simple physical movements I used to take for granted is a true gift.

Many challenges and obstacles present an opportunity to be better and not bitter. I am a better human being because of osteoporosis. I occasionally think about "what if" I did not have to worry about my compromised bones. When grounded and grateful, I am lucky to be alive and healthy with *only* osteoporosis.

Osteoporosis helped me take the high road regarding my attitude and how I treat people. I am more sensitive to others with physical challenges then I ever was before. None of us knows when our time is up on earth. As we discussed in chapter two, we never know when life's insurmountable challenges transform us. We not only live through these obstacles, they may change our life forever. Has there been a life-changing event for you? What challenges are you currently facing? Which tools will you deploy for assistance in taking the high road when a life challenge overwhelms you?

Taking the high road is an attitude: an attitude of gratitude. Moreover, it's a state of being: peaceful, confident, empathetic, humble, selfless, and understanding a broader perspective. It is not weakness. A true sign of self-confidence is to use each tool when taking the high road. Dad had a tool belt he wore every day at work. We all have tool belts. They wrap our hearts, minds, and physical bodies.

When we effectively use our tools, each is positioned to help us take the high road routinely. The first tool, *Paying Attention*, leads to self-awareness and the ability to take the high road. Leading our thoughts with a high-road mindset can begin the process of *Forgiveness*, our fifth tool. When we *Utilize Goals* (second tool) they should be SMART goals (specific, measurable, achievable, realistic, and time-sensitive) to take the high road. Tool number four, *Daily Reflection*, asks the question at the end of the day, "Did I take the high road today?" *Starting Simply* (tool three) begins with the intention to start taking the high road daily. In what category of our life can we *Start Simply* and be successful in high-road behaviors? Pick a life category and start now.

Life's challenges and obstacles are the barometer for taking the high road. It is easy to take the high road when we have had a productive day, had a few small victories, and life did not present any significant challenges or obstacles to overcome. However, the most critical time we need the key to our belt (taking the high road) is when life presents obstructions, hardships, and confrontations that appear insurmountable. This is when all our tools need to be unleashed and executed.

In our last chapter, we will sharpen all our tools, and the result is being *good tired* at the end of each day.

CHAPTER NINE

Good Tired

How to get off the treadmill of life and escape the race to nowhere is an ongoing challenge we face each day. When we are *good tired*, we actively participate in a unique contest in which we decide the rules. Our playbook is the tool kit we developed. All our tools (*Pay Attention, Utilize Goals, Start Simply, Reflect Daily, Forgive*) are imperative for us to experience *good tired* at the end of each day.

In the previous chapters, we utilized the dictionary to define specific words: "purpose," "attention," "goal," "reflect," "forgiveness," and "high road." However, there is no definition of *good tired* in the dictionary.

What does *good tired* mean to Mike Lauesen? This question has been implicitly present throughout the book and is one of the fundamental impetuses for me writing this book. Thinking through the question, "What does *good tired* mean?" has been integral to my own process of self-discovery, exploration, and meaning of life.

Good tired is when we wake up each morning and know why we are here on this earth. This *why* can help lead us to our purpose in life. As we discussed in Chapter two, "Uncovering Your Life Purpose," revealing and understanding your purpose is a challenge. It is often conceived through the joys and sorrows of our life journey. This occurred for me when two of my older sisters experienced life-changing events in the late 1980s. It reverberated throughout all our extended families. Because of these experiences, my purpose was revealed. Today, I can unequivocally say that this life-changing experience was the catalyst which helped unveil my life's fundamental purpose. For Mike Lauesen, it is to give back all the love I have received and make a positive difference in the life of every person I meet. If I follow my purpose, I will be *good tired*. Many folks know their purpose at an early age and some have yet to discover it. Reviewing chapter two may help uncover your purpose or validate it, and in turn allow you to be *good tired*.

Following our own moral compass and values with personal integrity, we sleep well, and *good tired* surrounds us. Living a life of integrity is not always popular or easy. We are faced with temptation each and every day. When we live with integrity, our personal values become part of our minds, hearts, and physical actions. We know with conviction to be steadfast for equality, justice, and fairness in the world. Then, we are *good tired*.

Let us expand the familiar intimacy of this conversation by invoking a distant and historical global set of events. Great Britain and the Allies fought World

War II against Nazi Germany to maintain freedom and democracy. All citizens understood the distinct possibility of potentially thousands of deaths and a loss of freedom. Freedom implies an enormous responsibility to fight for a worthy cause and live or die with the consequences. This is *good tired* in life and death. This historically potent moment reveals the common thread of *good tired* in the public sphere.

What are your personal values? If you practice, defend, and act on your values, you will be *good tired*.

Good tired entails following our dreams. Dreams can become goals, and those goals can become reality. We strive for our dreams and goals through hard work, dedication, perseverance, a great attitude, and enjoying the journey. *Good tired* is not about achieving our wildest dreams, but delighting in the adventure.

So, let us start here. Effort is compulsory in feeling *Good tired*. We are resolved to do what is necessary when we encounter adversity and significant challenges. It is not about "winning." It is about faith and courage. We must have conviction followed by dedicated actionable behaviors. *Good tired* suggests after all is said and done, more is *done* than said. In an earlier chapter, we reflected on the process Bob Richards discussed: we pay the price by doing the work. Our effort and actions cannot be in question. This commitment to effort must be unwavering.

Let us think through a couple of examples from

American history. Abraham Lincoln was undoubtedly *good tired* after the Gettysburg address. The speech was given November 19, 1863, four-and-a-half months after 51,000 men died on the battlefield. Can you imagine the hallowed and haunted feeling President Lincoln felt as he began his speech at Gettysburg? The speech was a little over two minutes long. Yet it has become one of the most iconic speeches in the history of our country, in which he proclaimed the Civil War as a struggle for preserving the union and for the principle of human equality. Lincoln was *good tired* when he announced this truth. He was unapologetic and his prophetic words were infused with steadfast courage and conviction.

Similarly, Martin Luther King Jr. was surely *good tired* after his historic and momentous "I Have a Dream" speech, 100 years later, from the steps of the Lincoln Memorial in Washington, DC. His speech to over 250,000 people on August 28, 1963, called for an end to racism and equality in civil and economic rights for citizens regardless of the color of their skin, race, or ethnicity. Abraham Lincoln and Martin Luther King Jr. demonstrated uncompromising effort, resolve, and integrity during extremely troubling times. Their foundation was a stable, enduring moral compass of fairness and equality for all humankind. Under those daunting, turbulent, and challenging times, they both personified being *good tired*.

Both of these inspirational leaders remind me of Teddy Roosevelt's "Man in the Arena." For me, it is a compelling and illustrative example of *good tired*. Here is the quote from Teddy Roosevelt:

"It is not the critic who counts; not the man who points out how the strong man stumbles, or where the doer of deeds could have done them better. The credit belongs to the man who is actually in the arena, whose face is marred by dust and sweat and blood; who strives valiantly; who errs, who comes short again and again, because there is no effort without error and shortcoming; but who does actually strive to do the deeds; who knows great enthusiasms, the great devotions; who spends himself in a worthy cause; who at the best knows in the end the triumph of high achievement, and who at the worst, if he fails, at least fails while daring greatly, so that his place shall never be with those cold and timid souls who neither know victory nor defeat."

What if we all dared greatly in every aspect of life, not only to be in the arena, but also to be *good tired* most days of our lives?

Do you want to be *good tired* at the end of each day? What do you want for your loved ones? Does this apply to the end of your life? How do we know if we are *good tired*? If we are not *good tired*, are we bad tired?

Let me expand on how and why to be *good tired* each day. When we are trapped on the treadmill, *good tired* is not an option. It is elusive. We can chase it, but the race is lost before we start. I have been trapped on the treadmill of life several times in my lifetime. How about you?

The most recent for me was in February, 2015. It lasted several disturbing months. Self-induced, I was solely responsible for being trapped.

Overloaded with responsibilities, activities, and duties in both my personal and professional life, I was trapped "being too busy." I felt unsettled and many nights fell asleep bad tired. My time was precious and always fleeing. I was moderator (highest elected lay person) of my local church, facilitating two CEO Vistage groups (Vistage is a peer advisory think tank for CEOs, presidents, and business owners), meeting every month for a ninety-minute coaching session with thirty different business leaders, writing a book, and attempting to be a caring and thoughtful dad, husband, and friend. I could barely write all of that in one sentence. I think you get the point. I was failing in most areas. Every category in my life wheel seemed hazy and unfulfilling. It was not possible to accomplish everything in a 168-hour week.

This overload had me frazzled, stressed out, and miserable. Trying to do too much, I was doing a poor job in each area. The 168 hours were neither balanced nor focused on what I believe is the most important category in life: relationships. My daughter Erin and I had a compelling conversation during this time. As she listened to my ramblings and all the things I was trying to accomplish, she finally interrupted and made an emphatic statement: "Dad, Dad; *get off the treadmill.*"

I felt her profound statement echo throughout my entire body. I was speechless. Looking back, it was a God moment. Was Mike Lauesen on the treadmill and racing to nowhere? It was immensely ironic. I was writing about getting off the treadmill and needed my wise daughter to jolt me out of my sleepwalking trance to nowhere.

Eventually letting go of some of the responsibilities and activities in both my career and church, I actively stopped my own race to nowhere, got off the treadmill, and focused on *good tired* as an outcome when I slept each night.

Have you recently been trapped on the treadmill and bad tired? What kinds of things in your life are contributing to this overwhelming burden? How would you rate your own relationship to *good tired*? These are not easy questions, and often answers may take time to unfold and courage to address.

What other ways can we be *good tired*? We are *good tired* when we are cognizant we have all the tools readily available. Utilizing each tool as needed throughout the day, *good tired* is the gauge we use before we fall asleep. Good tired is our daily guide to determine if we were mindful of our purpose. Did we jump on the treadmill during the day? If you are on the treadmill, make the choice to get off now.

Starting simply, tool number three is the first step to be *good tired*. Reflect on the wheel or categories of life. Perhaps start with your intention to be *good tired* at the end of each day with your family. This intention will provide more awareness regarding *good tired*. What can you accomplish daily with your own family to be *good tired*? Ask your family, "What is the most important thing needed in your life to feel *good tired*?" If we *Pay Attention*, focus on, and support our families, this will undoubtedly contribute to our own *good tired*.

If we *Start Simply* with our purpose in life, it can be our guidepost to start reflecting every day. Ask yourself a question at the end of the day: "Did I accomplish part of my life's mission and am I *good tired* because of it?"

This kind of self-awareness is bolstered as we focus on the present by paying attention. Are we *Paying Attention* (our first tool) to what is important in life to us? When we are not paying attention, we miss things we are not even aware of. It is not only the first law of spirituality according to Pastor Doug Runnells; it is the most critical tool for *good tired,* as all the other tools are sharpened when we *Pay Attention* well.

We tap into the divine and God moments when we *Pay Attention* and are open to the creator. Someone (maybe God) or your children reminds us to *Pay Attention*, get off the treadmill, and grants *good tired* when we sleep. How and what do you *Pay Attention* to and avow *good tired* most nights when you lay your head down to sleep?

SMART goals are necessary to be *good tired*. When we *Utilize Goals* (tool two), it makes an impactful difference in our life. Although I had goals before I listened to Bob Richards speak in college, his talk on motivation and goals was transformational. Following Bob Richards' four steps (utilize goals, paying the price, feeling you deserve great things to happen to you, and understanding the outcome may not always be realized) we learn the journey is critical in both goal-setting and in the rhythms of life. By enjoying the journey, we are often in a flow state and have a higher likelihood of being *good tired*. We are not attached to the outcome of our goals. We understand there is always a lesson in the voyage versus the acquiring of the goal.

What is your method of *daily reflection?* How do you remind yourself to dream toward *good tired*: gratefulness, breath, meditation, rituals, thin places and God moments, other methods? Tool number four, *Reflect Daily*, provides awareness and techniques on how to be *good tired* at the end of each day. Good tired is an experience we can all share. Slowing down to reflect on *good tired*, we can determine two things: are we bad tired or *good tired*? I want many more *good tired* days than any other kind of tired. A daily reflection can reset our barometer of *good tired*.

When we practice *Forgiveness* (last tool), we not only take the *High Road*, we are also working toward *good tired*. Forgiveness and *good tired* are symbiotic, and both provide us opportunities to get off the treadmill and the race to nowhere. Forgiveness magnifies our feeling of *good tired*. The liberation we receive from the act of forgiveness is a key attribute of feeling and being *good tired*. How does forgiveness lead us to *good tired*? Let me personally reflect a few stories here.

Forgiving myself for allowing Conor to be abused was a long process. *Good tired* was not fully realized until I took responsibility as a father for what happened. Once I asked Conor for forgiveness, the pain in my heart and soul gradually subsided. Conor and I could not change the past. Moving beyond the past released my heartache and allowed me to experience *good tired*. Do you need to forgive yourself for something that is holding you back from moving on with your life? How does this relate to *good tired* for you?

Family, friends, and others have demonstrated a powerful influence on my life. They have taught me love, wisdom, and lessons. The most important is how to experience and live a life being *good tired*.

As I have mentioned, my dad, Howard Lauesen, was a lather by trade. There is artistry in lathing. He took tremendous pride and loved his work. Dad built archways in shopping centers, beautiful homes, entranceways in buildings, and interiors of hospitals. Working in the extreme cold, windy winters and hot, humid summers of Chicago was part of the job description. Dad was physically exhausted when he arrived home, yet was *good tired*. *Good tired* is not about physical fatigue. How many people do we all know who at the end of the day are physically drained, but still feel empty, lacking the depth of *good tired*?

My dad, Howard, is an example I would like to further share. Dad not only immersed himself in the seriousness and care of his craft; he also reflected daily about his work. Although I do not remember Dad ever stating he was *Reflecting Daily*, (tool number four), he did, every day. He practiced gratitude regarding his life's work without ever stating it. Dad was grateful. He was humbled to have work and took pride in giving all his effort to his job.

Working a summer during college as a laborer for the company my dad worked for, I was able to see him in action. Howard Lauesen had one gear—a very high gear. He efficiently produced exceptional work and received enormous fulfillment and happiness from a hard day's work. He never wanted to be an owner, a superintendent, or even a foreman. He was happy and fulfilled as a journeyman lather, doing the work he did every day, and taking daily pride in his work. Dad reflected daily with gratitude and pride in his work output.

It is difficult to imagine lacking passion and love for what you do for a living. While many jobs may prove challenging, and ideal work is not always available, we all continue to have choices. Attitude and effort can help all of us strive through the day and we can each focus more on genuine engagement and good mental exhaustion even when one's job opportunities may seem stagnant and frustrating. *Good tired* is available for all of us. The lessons learned from Dad are inside my heart: love your work, be passionate, take pride in it, and be grateful. If you do that most days, it will be a good day. My dad slept well every night because he was *good tired*.

Now I want to tell you a different story about a dear friend. Manuel Gamboa was the first employee of Nicoat. When we started Nicoat, I never imagined the deep friendship we would develop. Manny (as he is commonly known) has grown with Nicoat over his thirty-two-year tenure. Learning, maturing, and growing as a businessman, husband, and father, I am proud to call him a friend. I would often say to colleagues, friends, and family, "If my son Conor grew up to be like Manny, I would be a fortunate and blessed father." Manny and Hilda (his wife) have three beautiful teenage daughters, Gabriella, Emily, and Rebecca. The entire Lauesen family is very proud of Manny because of his dedication to his loving family and many accomplishments at Nicoat.

Manny has been *good tired* as long as I have known him. He is *good tired* because he is grounded and focused on our first tool, *Paying Attention*. As you may recall, paying attention is the foundation of all our tools. It was our Pastor's first law of spirituality. Growing up with parents who were born in Mexico, he learned his values from seeing and doing within his family. As second-oldest in a family of five, Manny realized how fortunate he was in America and paid attention.

His uncompromising ethics and moral compass is unwavering. His integrity could never be questioned. I am privileged and honored to have worked with him for twenty-five years; my love and respect for Manny is steadfast and enduring.

Turning fifty years of age recently, Manny has been at Nicoat his entire business career. Manny has worked in almost every department or function. He started helping in the laboratory, learned how to formulate products and was a batch maker in production. He eventually managed the lab and the plant. Paying attention to each and every role prepared him for his current role as Chief Operating Officer. He has had three bosses in his entire career and learned from each one because of his gift of paying attention. His current boss, the CEO of Nicoat, feels the same sentiment as I do.

Why is this? One of the primary reasons is because Manny is *good tired* and constantly pays attention. He does all the right things every day: he is productive in his job, respectful of his peers and folks who work for him, and cares about the customers. Manny follows the same behaviors at home. Going the extra mile is an everyday occurrence with Manny Gamboa. He is consistently consistent.

Dedicated and loving to his family, combined with his uncompromising commitment to Nicoat, he epitomizes work-life balance. He pays attention to all the important things in life. His balanced life has not only been greatly influenced by his intrinsic character and career, but also because of his familial traditions tied to his own background as a Mexican-American. Manny has worked hard in all categories of his own Wheel of Life. His focus is on relationships: his family, customers and colleagues of Nicoat, and his church. They are the cornerstone and foundation of Manny's life. He is a doer, not a talker. I am grateful to have worked with him, and to have developed a friendship beyond Nicoat. Like my dad, and hopefully you, Manny is *good tired* most days.

This last example reflects on a public figure, a man who many of us may be familiar with. Jimmy Valvano, the famous college basketball coach, won the National College Basketball Championship in 1983. Under improbable odds, his team, North Carolina State (Wolfpack) defeated the University of Houston (Cougars). The Cougars had won twenty-six games in a row until they lost to the Wolfpack in the Championship.

Jimmy V (as he was affectionately known) continued coaching till 1991 and then went into broadcasting. Sadly, he contracted bone cancer in June of 1992.

He died of cancer April 28, 1993, at the age of forty-seven. His wife and three daughters survive him.

In his famous ESPY's speech, March 3, 1993, Jimmy V announced: "Never give up, never give up." He shared the following: "When people say to me, 'How do you get through life or each day,' it's the same thing. To me, there are three things we all should do every day. Number one is laugh. You should laugh every day. Number two is think. You should spend some time in thought. Number three is you should have your emotions moved to tears, could be happiness or joy. But think about it. If you laugh, you think, and you cry, that's a full day. That's a heck of a day. You do that seven days a week, you're going to have something special." Jimmy V was *good tired*. He was *good tired* when he laughed, spent time in thought, and had his emotions moved.

At the end of his momentous speech, Coach Valvano discussed time. Time was precious to him, as he didn't know how much time he had left. He wanted to give hope for others with cancer. He announced with the help of ESPN, they were starting the V Foundation for Cancer Research. The motto is: "Don't Give Up…Don't Ever Give Up!" Even near death, Jimmy V discovered a new purpose in life (chapter two—Uncovering Your Life Purpose) by creating a new charitable foundation dedicated to saving lives by helping find a cure for cancer.

Jimmy V's three things (laugh, think, cry) make up a good day and are significant to me and countless others. They epitomize our third tool, *Starting Simply*. A good day simply started with only three things to accomplish: laugh, think, and cry. This simple formula can help lead us to being *good tired* every day. Coach Valvano chased his dreams, fought his own battles, and slept well at night. He was *good tired*.

My first job out of college, as an accounting major, was with Ernst and Whinney (now Ernst & Young). A year later, after passing the C.P.A. exam, I was a Certified Public Accountant. After two years as an auditor, I was very unsatisfied and decided to leave the profession. Telling Barbara and my parents I was leaving accounting was a milestone in my career. Barbara understood I was unhappy, despite the great financial career accounting affords. She was, however, excited for whatever my new career might be. The conversation with my parents was quite different. Dad incredulously looked at me and asked, "Why would you go to college, become an accountant, get your C.P.A., and then leave your career?" As I mentioned earlier in this chapter, Dad worked as a lather. He worked his craft throughout his whole working life until he retired. He did not understand the idea of a career change I was contemplating. Explaining to him as best I could, I said my work was unsatisfying and I had lost my passion. Although it was a learning experience and paid well, *good tired* was out of my reach.

My next job, with NCR Corporation, was selling computer software and hardware for three years. It was an excellent job, both rewarding and challenging. I thoroughly enjoyed calling on prospects, developing new customers, and exceeding sales goals. My three years were fun; I was learning every day in a dynamic environment, exceeding goals, and being rewarded while earning a hefty paycheck. Yet something was missing.

For a long while I had a dream of owning my own business before the age of thirty. More than anything else, I wanted the opportunity to control my own destiny. My goal (second tool) did not have a specific business in mind. At the time, a close friend of mine, Mike Sullivan, was self-employed. He was a role model and mentor for me. Many nights we discussed how and why he had started his own business. Mike was an inspiration and his help was integral to me eventually figuring out a way to get started in my own business. Today we are still friends and often reminisce about the early days of our careers and our first meeting at a Toastmasters International meeting.

In 1985, I was twenty-eight years of age, married, with a one-year-old (my son Conor) living in Glenview, Illinois, in a small two-bedroom ranch home. That year I started Nicoat with my father-in-law, John. He had a chemical and paint background. As a result, we believed we would be in the industrial paint business. It did not quite work out the way we planned.

It was a God moment when I reluctantly attended my ten-year high school reunion shortly after we incorporated Nicoat. All of us attending wanted to know what each other did for a living. We passed out cards and learned about each other after high school or college. This is where I reconnected with a grammar-school classmate, Ron Schneider. He worked as a pressman at American Printers and Lithographers. They were a commercial printer down the street from where I lived. Asking Ron if they used any coatings, he answered, "Yes, we use water-based coatings on the JC Penney catalogs."

Ron, without knowing it, helped develop my vision for the company. The vision was very simple. Living in Chicago, I discovered hundreds of printers within a four-hundred-mile radius who needed coatings, either at that point or in the near future. Within months, we began to manufacture clear overprint coatings for the printing industry.

Starting and building Nicoat into a multi-million-dollar international specialty-coating company was fulfilling. Throughout the entire process, it was challenging, rewarding, and fun. Although it was seven long years before we turned a profit, we were creating something special with each other at work and with our customers. It was a spectacular team effort. Although I am no longer involved with Nicoat, I am proud my colleagues and friends are still working together at Nicoat. The relationships and friendships we built together have lasted until this day.

~

My family has always been my highest priority.

When I see folks spending more time in their careers than with their families, it makes me sad. Would we realistically want to say during our last moments alive, "I wish I would've worked harder and longer hours?"

Do you spend enough time with your loved ones?

Making some very deliberate and conscious choices in the early years of my business, I wanted a manageable work-life balance. I traveled no more than two nights a week for business and worked very few weekends. Barbara and I raised four children who are now adults. Could I have put more hours in on weekends or evenings as we built and grew the business? Absolutely. Yet somehow I knew getting the time back with my family would never happen. I wanted to be *good tired* from work and at home.

This seems to be missed in today's culture of 24/7 availability for work. If we can financially make it work, actually spending time, not just "quality time," with our loved ones while having a career is a conscious choice.

Making time for coaching my kids was important to me. It was a magical time in our lives and worth every practice and game coached in baseball or soccer. It was frantic and hectic most weeks. Barbara and I created a schedule one spring for all of the kids' activities. Each of our kids was involved with one or two sports. The calendar was full every day with practices and games. As I was the coach in baseball and soccer, we soon realized attending all the practices and games was impossible. We tore the schedule up and juggled it all as best as possible. Upon later reflection, I guess we made a conscious choice to be *good tired*.

Experiencing *good tired* most Sunday nights was pleasing, gratifying, and fulfilling. Maybe I lost the prior week. Possibly we lost a customer during the week, the new product launch failed, or lost the game I coached, but I was *good tired*, and settled easy into bed and slept well.

~

Do you love what you do? Do you need to change your career?

Do you care enough about your life outside of your career? Reflect on the time you spend in the categories in your own life. Can you change your focus in your categories of life?

If you did focus on other important facets of life, will this be the change you need to be *good tired*?

Good tired is available for all of us. What can you do to be *good tired* at the end of the day?

My first encounter with the term *good tired* was from Harry Chapin. Harry was a singer, songwriter, poet, activist, and philanthropist. For me, his music and storytelling resonate more today than ever. Harry was not on the treadmill. His race was ongoing with no finish line. He entered a race to make a permanent difference in the world through his music and his philanthropy.

Harry died in an automobile accident on July 16, 1981. He was thirty-eight years old. His wife, Sandy, their two children, Jen and Josh, and three adopted stepchildren, Jaime, Jonathan, and Jason, survived him. I cannot imagine the shock and sorrow this caused for his family.

At twenty-three years of age, it was a life-changing event for me. Barbara and I felt like we lost a close friend whom we had known throughout our young lives.

We became lifelong fans after attending a Harry Chapin concert in high school. His passionate, lively, humorous, sad, and poignant stories of ordinary folk's joys, sorrows, trials, and tribulations in life inspired and deeply touched our souls. We met Harry several times after the many concerts we attended. Harry was fully engaged, paying attention to each and every fan he met. He sold Harry Chapin shirts, a poetry book, and other items of interest, with all proceeds helping eradicate world hunger. He is still our favorite singer, songwriter, and storyteller.

Although Harry never knew us by name, he is one of the most influential people in my life. Our kids have listened to Harry's songs, live recordings, taped conversations, and interviews. His wisdom, passion, and voice speak loudly in our home today.

As committed, devoted, and faithful fans, we listened to his music at home, attended concerts, and waited with joy and anticipation when a new album was released. When Harry died, we lost more than a musician and entertainer. We lost someone who exemplified *good tired* most days of his life.

Despite his brief life, all he accomplished demonstrated his passion, love of life, and the belief we all can make an impactful difference in the world. His accolades and achievements are numerous. Here are a few:

- The Harry Chapin Foundation

- Why Hunger (formerly World Hunger Year)

- Posthumously awarded a Special Congressional Gold Medal

- Nominated for an Oscar in documentary filmmaking for *Legendary Champions*.

He performed hundreds of sold-out concerts a year where half the proceeds were donated to World Hunger Year. He had several songs in the *Billboard* Top 40 chart ("Taxi," "Circle," "WOLD") and a number one hit in "Cat's in the Cradle."

Several years after Harry died, old and new recordings were released. One significant recording to me was an interview with Harry about his grandfather. His grandfather was in his eighties when he shared *good tired* and *bad tired* with Harry.

"My grandfather was a painter. He died at age eighty-eight, he illustrated Robert Frost's first two books of poetry, and he was looking at me and he said, 'Harry, there's two kinds of tired. There's *good tired* and there's bad tired.' He said, 'Ironically enough, bad tired can be a day that you won. But you won other people's battles; you lived other people's days, other people's agendas, and other people's dreams. And when it's all over, there was very little you in there. And when you hit the hay at night, somehow you toss and turn; you don't settle easy. It's that *good tired*, ironically enough, can be a day that you lost, but you don't even have to tell yourself because you knew you fought your battles, you chased your dreams, you lived your days and when you hit the hay at night, you settle easy, you sleep the sleep of the just and you say, take me away.' He said, 'Harry, all my life I wanted to be a painter and I painted; God, I would have loved to have been more successful, but I painted and I painted and I'm *good tired* and they can take me away.'"

Harry's grandfather articulates the message in such a beautiful way.

We have covered a lot of ground in our chase to the end of this book. My race included being trapped on the treadmill and recently getting off. Through this writing odyssey, you know more about my wife, kids, parents, philosophy, career, and mentors than some of my close friends.

You have traveled this quest with me, hopefully to say goodbye to the treadmill of life. By harnessing all you have learned, you can optimistically and trustingly move forward with confidence to your desired destination. Whether it is the race to stronger relationships; paying attention to life's simple pleasures; going to your peaceful, quiet place; or discovering God moments or your core purpose; may your journey with your tool kit always be the foundation of your life to be *good tired*, each and every day. Hopefully, *good tired* becomes part of you as it is for me. I trust we will be off the treadmill and *good tired* when the race ends with our last breath.

The Final Inning,

Mike

"Oh, if a man tried to take his time on earth and prove before he died what one man's life could be worth I wonder what would happen to this world"

HARRY CHAPIN

APPENDIX

Your Tool Kit

TOOL A: Your Own Funeral

1. Decide the four people who will speak at your funeral (Family member, close friend, colleague from your career, a member of your place of worship or civic organization).

   a. Family Member: _____

   b. Close Friend: _____

   c. Career Colleague: _____

   d. Worship Place/Civic Organization:

   _____

2. Write what each person will say about you.

   a. Family Member: _____

   _____

   _____

   _____

   _____

   _____

b. Close Friend: Career Colleague: _____

_____

_____

_____

_____

_____

_____

_____

c. Worship Place/Civic Organization: _____

_____

_____

_____

_____

_____

3. Below is a vertical line and two horizontal lines. To the left of the vertical line, put the year you were born.

4. Now I want you to think about the year you will die. Is it twenty, thirty, or perhaps forty years or more from today? Envision a ripe old age of ninety, 100, or beyond. To the right of the second horizontal line, write the year you think you will die.

_____ | _____

5. In the space below titled "Life So Far," list your most satisfying accomplishments and experiences, both personally and professionally. Itemize your biggest disappointments. Take your time; there are no correct answers.

Life So Far _____

_____

_____

_____

_____

6. In the space below titled "The Time that Remains," begin to write what you hope to have experienced and/or accomplished. A few examples might be: births of grandchildren, getting married or remarried, vacations you will take, relocating to a new home and or city, becoming an entrepreneur, or retiring with a specific age in mind. Make note of why this is important to you. It is critical to write your thoughts on the above, as this enables you to uncover your purpose for the remaining time we have here on earth.

The Time that Remains_____

_____

_____

_____

_____

TOOL B: What I Do in My Free Time

TOOL C: What I Care About

_____

_____

_____

_____

_____

_____

_____

_____

_____

_____

_____

_____

_____

_____

_____

_____

_____

_____

_____

_____

_____

_____

TOOL D: Paying Attention and the Alpha State

Follow each step, in order. You are now starting a coaching lesson.

1. Write all the ways you currently *Pay Attention* during your waking hours.

_____

_____

_____

_____

_____

_____

_____

2. Write the activities that allow you to experience alpha or "flow."

_____

_____

_____

_____

_____

_____

_____

3. Take a deep breath. Imagine your peaceful, quiet place. (When you first imagine your peaceful, quiet place, it is the first place that comes to your mind. Trust your first thought or your intuition.) Describe and write the place. Create written details around your peaceful, quiet place.

_____

_____

_____

_____

_____

_____

_____

_____

4. Practice daily, paying attention during your waking hours, and go to your peaceful, quiet place (alpha state) six to twelve times a day. Twenty seconds is all you need.

5. Create daily reminders for yourself to remember to go to alpha. This could be when you drink water; transitioning from standing and/or sitting to walking; when you enter your car, or the train on your commute. Before you eat or go to bed is also a good reminder to go to alpha.

TOOL E: SMART GOALS

Follow each step in order.

1. Reflect on and write three goals you achieved in high school, college, or your first job.

    a. _____

    b. _____

    c. _____

2. Write three personal and/or career goals for the next twelve months.

    a. _____

    b. _____

    c. _____

3. Evaluate whether these are SMART goals. Rewrite them if necessary.

4. Place copies of your written SMART goals where you can see them every day. Maybe on your kitchen table, your phone, car, a mirror in your bathroom.

5. Twice a week, spend fifteen minutes thinking about your goals.

6. Develop a scoring system you can track monthly. This is designed to determine if are you on track or behind in achieving your goals. The system I use is red, yellow, and green. Red is behind on your goal or losing; yellow is no progress since last tracked, and green is meeting your goal or winning.

7. Once a month, assess your scoring system and make adjustments to stay on course for meeting your short term, annual, or longer-term goal.

TOOL F: Life Categories and Priorities

1. Review the Life Categories/Wheel of Life; feel free to add your own categories, modify, or use what I provided.

2. Write the approximate time you currently spend in each category or grouping.

    Family _____

    Relationships _____

    Spirituality _____

    Career _____

    Finances _____

    Travel _____

    Health: physical, mental, emotional _____

    Leisure, relaxation _____

3. Write your SMART goal for number of hours in each section or category.

    Family _____

    Relationships _____

    Spirituality _____

    Career _____

    Finances _____

    Travel _____

    Health: physical, mental, emotional _____

    Leisure, relaxation _____

4. Fill in the number of hours you have free time.

_____

_____

_____

_____

5. List what you *want* to do with your free time.

_____

_____

_____

_____

6. Pay attention to what you currently do versus what you *want* to do in your "spare time."

7. Create a SMART goal for your own "sixty hours" of time outside of work, commuting, and sleeping. *Start Simply*, with the first line of your SMART goal: "I will spend ___ hours per week doing the following...."

_____

_____

_____

_____

8. Determine who your coach or coaches will be. Meet with your coach at least monthly to assist you in accomplishing your goals.

TOOL G: Reflect Daily—Gratefulness

Follow each step, in order.

1. List what you are grateful for.

    The following may help you get started: reading, working out, good health, growing up with freedoms in America, sleep, family, friends, mentors, vacations, money, giving to charities, grocery stores, medical care, and regular work. Make sure you include basic needs such as shelter, food, water, walking, seeing, and hearing. Your list should provide a multitude of things to be grateful for.

    _____

    _____

    _____

    _____

    _____

    _____

    _____

    _____

    _____

    _____

    _____

    _____

    _____

    _____

2. For one week, add to your list each morning.

   Day 1: _____

   Day 2: _____

   Day 3: _____

   Day 4: _____

   Day 5: _____

   Day 6: _____

   Day 7: _____

3. Review the list daily.

TOOL H: Reflect Daily—Breath

Follow each step, in order.

1. Be in a quiet place, sit, and relax.

2. Close your eyes.

3. Take three deep breaths through your nose only. Inhaling through your nose, breathe into your belly and let the air fill up your lungs. On the exhale (through your nose or mouth), let your body round forward a little as the air empties out of you and gently squeeze your abdomen at the end of the exhale.

4. Pay attention to your body and how it feels. Relax each limb.

5. Repeat this activity three to four times a day for a month. It may become a habit.

TOOL I: Forgiveness

1. Write the names of people you want to forgive.

_____

_____

_____

_____

_____

_____

_____

_____

_____

2. Write the names of people who you feel need forgiveness for something you have done.

_____

_____

_____

_____

_____

_____

_____

_____

_____

3. Reflect on Desmond Tutu's four steps: A) Tell the story, B) Name the hurt, C) Grant forgiveness, D) Renew or release the relationship, event or circumstances.

4. Select one of the names you want to forgive.

_____

5. Share the story with a close friend, therapist, or whomever you are comfortable with.

6. Reflect about this person and the circumstances of what they did to you. It will help you fully understand why you need to forgive them.

7. Name the hurt and write your emotions and feelings.

_____

_____

_____

_____

_____

_____

_____

_____

_____

_____

8. Can you grant forgiveness yet? If so, determine how you will proceed. Will you do this alone, or will you share this with the perpetrator?

9. Can you renew or release the relationship? If so, choose to renew or release the relationship.

10. Remind yourself forgiveness is a lifelong process and at times is difficult. The four steps are not linear.

ABOUT THE AUTHOR

Mike Lauesen is a lifelong learner and student. Mike's purpose in life is to make an impactful, positive difference in every life he touches. He was greatly influenced by his upbringing. He grew up with seven brothers and sisters in a modest three-bedroom ranch-style home with one bathroom. He worked several jobs in high school, learning the value of hard work from his parents and older siblings.

While attending the University of Minnesota on an athletic scholarship, he learned invaluable life lessons one summer selling cutlery door-to-door. After graduation, Mike started his career in accounting (a recovered C.P.A.), then sold computers and software and eventually founded his own specialty chemical/coating company (Nicoat) in 1985 at twenty-eight years of age. After building Nicoat into a successful professionally managed international company, he exited as founder/CEO and started a new career as a professional speaker and life coach.

He is passionate, funny, and entertaining as a professional speaker. Mike is a Competent Toastmaster (International Speaking Association) and coaches/mentors business leaders or anyone who is a ready student.

Mike wrote *Getting off the Treadmill* because he wanted to change people's lives for the better. His main message is, "Don't live your life in a sleepwalking trance." Instead, be aware of all the joys life has to offer. As a result of these pages, he hopes you'll find more personal insights, more life direction, more happiness, and use the tools included to improve the quality of your life.

He is married to Dr. Barbara Lauesen and has four adult children (Conor, Erin, Cailie, and Taylor) who are all involved in social justice causes and education. Mike humbly states, "Without my wife and children, I could never live and experience such a charmed and grateful life." Mike enjoys, reading, cycling, travel, the Chicago Cubs, and spending time with his family.

To inquire about booking Mike Lauesen as a speaker or bulk book discounts, please e-mail mlauesen@gmail.com or call 847-922-6162.

ACKNOWLEDGMENTS

Thank you to my wife Barbara, my best friend since high school. She is my biggest fan, a daily inspiration, and a great editor and writer. Barbara had many great ideas such as making baseball part of this book. Barbara understands my love and passion for the game. She has been supportive from the beginning through editing.

My kids have been wonderful. They all cared and gave me amazing edits, ideas, and motivated me to finish the book. Conor intensely read each chapter and provided ideas and many insights. The use of metaphors for my Dad's tools was Conor's idea.

Erin challenged me several times in her comments and made many great suggestions, including getting off the treadmill. Cailie kept me grounded and reminded me I could do this and believed it would be great. Taylor, our baby, shared much wisdom and love, and listened incredibly well to me reading out loud. She also provided me the idea of the tool kit.

Henry DeVries of Indie Books International, my editor and publisher, is where everything started. I can remember his first question: "Why do you want to write a book?" He guided, inspired, motivated, coached, and kept me on track and off the treadmill to eventually finish the book.

I worked with Joann Dobbie as a book mentor. Thank goodness I found her through another editor/publisher, Susie Isaac. After our first meeting, I knew I had received a tremendous gift. Joann helped me become a better writer over time. She was always sensitive to my ability, yet wanted me to grow as a writer and challenged me countless times. Her expert coaching kept me on schedule and inspired me. One provocative, daunting, and motivating suggestion was to consider what my grandson Luke would think of this book when he went to college (he is now thirteen months old).

Harry Chapin: He will never know the impact he has had on my life and my family and friends. Harry is a gift that keeps giving. Thank you, Harry; I only wish you lived longer.

Thank you to my parents, Blanche and Howard. You loved me and wanted me to reach beyond my farthest dreams. You both always believed in me.

My appreciation for my seven siblings is far-reaching. I have learned so many lessons, it is hard to keep track. Thank you, Chrissy, my oldest sister, for your comments and suggestions in reading a final draft and to Mary for the idea of the retractable tape measure.

I am appreciative to Wini, a family friend, who had more confidence in me to write a book and speak about it than I did.

I am grateful to my proof readers of the galley, Wes Marsh and Vanessa Podgorski. Their insights, corrections, and kindness was wonderful.

I am very grateful to Reverend Bobbie McKay, PhD. She read my manuscript with love and compassion. I will be forever changed through Bobbie's guidance in my own spiritual journey.

Thank you to longtime friend, Susie Walsh, who allowed me to tell such a personally tragic yet uplifting story. Whenever I think of Sue, I am inspired and feel I should be doing more to change the world.

I have told the story of listening to a speech of Bob Richards hundreds of times to different people throughout my whole life. You motivated me all those years ago to accomplish more than I could have ever imagined.

Thank you to TEC and Vistage for imbuing me with an insatiable desire to learn.

I am grateful for the authors in the works referenced pages and many, many others who helped shaped my thinking.

Finally, I want to thank our creator for the many God moments of inspiration and increasing my awareness of thin places.

WORKS REFERENCED

Baker, Dan, and Cameron Stauth. *What Happy People Know: How the New Science of Happiness Can Change Your Life for the Better*. Emmaus, PA: Rodale, 2003.

Bipp, Tanja, and Ad Kleingeld. "Goal-setting in Practice." Personnel Review 40, no. 3 (2011): 306-23. doi:10.1108/00483481111118630.

Borg, Marcus J. *The Heart of Christianity: Rediscovering a Life of Faith*. San Francisco: HarperSanFrancisco, 2003.

Brown, Brené. *I Thought It Was Just Me (but It Isn't): Telling the Truth about Perfectionism, Inadequacy, and Power*. New York: Gotham Books, 2008.

Carr, Nicholas G. *The Shallows: What the Internet Is Doing to Our Brains*. New York: W.W. Norton, 2010.

Collins, James C. *Good to Great: Why Some Companies Make the Leap ... and Others Don't*. New York, NY: HarperBusiness, 2001.

Covey, Stephen R. *The 7 Habits of Highly Effective People*. Provo, UT: Franklin Covey, 1998.

Csikszentmihalyi, Mihaly. *Flow: The Psychology of Optimal Experience*. New York: Harper & Row, 1990.

Halberstam, David. *Playing for Keeps: Michael Jordan and the World He Made*. New York: Random House, 1999.

Hicks, Donna, and Desmond Tutu. *Dignity: The Essential Role It Plays in Resolving Conflict*. New Haven: Yale University Press, 2011.

Hillenbrand, Laura. *Unbroken: A World War II Story of Survival, Resilience, and Redemption*. New York: Random House, 2010.

Kushner, Harold S. *When Bad Things Happen to Good People*. New York: Schocken Books, 1981.

Leman, Kevin. *Keeping Your Family Together When the World Is Falling Apart*. New York, NY: Delacorte Press, 1992.

Peck, M. Scott. *The Road Less Traveled: A New Psychology of Love, Traditional Values, and Spiritual Growth*. New York: Simon and Schuster, 1978.

Snyder, Steven. *Focused Passion: Become Better, Faster, Smarter and Happier With Far Less Stress and Much More Passion!* Hawaii: The Larry Czerwonka Company, 2014.

Tolle, Eckhart. *The Power of Now: A Guide to Spiritual Enlightenment*. Novato, CA: New World Library, 1999.

Tutu, Desmond, Douglas Abrams Carlton, and Mpho Tutu A. *The Book of Forgiving: The Fourfold Path for Healing Ourselves and Our World*. New York: HarperOne, 2014.

Van Der Kolk, Bessel A. *The Body Keeps the Score: Brain, Mind, and Body in the Healing of Trauma*. New York: Penguin Publishing Group, 2015.

Walsh, Susan Magnuson. *Walking in Broken Shoes: A Nurse's Story about Haiti and the Earthquake*. Larkspur, CO: Grace Acres Press, 2011.

Warren, Richard. *The Purpose-driven Life: What on Earth Am I Here For?* Grand Rapids, MI: Zondervan, 2002.

CPSIA information can be obtained
at www.ICGtesting.com
Printed in the USA
LVOW12*2045220517
535460LV00001BA/3/P